Books by E. J. Kahn, jr.

THE STRAGGLERS

THE
STRAGGLERS

E. J. KAHN, jr.

RANDOM HOUSE
New York

Most of the material in this book originally appeared, in somewhat different form, in The New Yorker, to which acknowledgment is gratefully made.

FIRST PRINTING

© Copyright, 1962, by E. J. KAHN, JR.

All rights reserved under International and Pan-American Copyright Conventions. Published in New York by Random House, Inc., and simultaneously in Toronto, Canada, by Random House of Canada, Limited.

Library of Congress Catalog Card Number: 62-17166

Manufactured in the United States of America by American Book–Stratford Press, Inc.

Design by Ruth Smerechniak

AUTHOR'S NOTE

The facts on which this book is based were largely gathered during a trip to the Far East in 1961. The book could not have been written without the patient cooperation of several of the former Japanese soldiers who, after hiding out for periods of from five to more than fifteen years, were fortunate enough to return to their homeland, and I wish to express my thanks herewith to Masao Akagi, Yuichi Akatsu, Kirachiro Funaba, Masashi Ito, Seiji Izumida, Keishichi Kishi, Bunzo Minagawa, Minoru Noda, Mamoru Ojima, Isamu Sakamoto, Tokio Samumatsu, Kakuo Shimada, Kumao Shimokubo, Haruo Tominaga, Yukimori Tsuda, and Shigeichi Yamamoto, and to the family of Sanzo Yaegashi.

Many others, in various parts of the world, helped out. Those to whom I owe a debt of thanks include Juan U. Aguon, Donald Bartlett, Keyes Beech, Cecil Brown, Isagani V. Campo, Harold C. Conklin, Jesse S. Cook, John De Young, Mary Jane Dom, Louis H. Engel, Jr., Alex Flores, Joseph Flores, Joseph Gorski, Stuart Griffin, Sakue Hirabayashi, T. Gordon Homme, S. Ikejima, Touru Itagaki, Nobuhiko Jimbo, Mock Joya, William Knapp, Leon M. Larson, Kiyoshi Makita, Yuzo Miura,

Keigo Okonogi, Toshio Onoda, Edward Quackenbush, Joaquin P. Roces, Sol Sanders, Faustino R. Sebastian, Tatsuo Shikano, Kiyoshi Sumiya, Hiroichi Tagawa, John and Toshiko Toland, Robert and Jean Trumbull, Edward G. Tsutsui, Nobuo Wakabayashi, and Wallace White.

Most of the relevant documents I consulted were in Japanese, a language with which, unhappily, I am not conversant. None of the ex-Japanese soldiers whom I interviewed or with whom I corresponded knew any English. It was thus necessary, for the major part of my research, to rely heavily upon translation and interpretation. For performing both these tasks in my behalf with diligence, intelligence, diplomacy, and skill, I am immeasurably obliged to my friend Yuzo Saita.

E.J.K.

Scarborough, New York
16 June 1962

�

CONTENTS

1

THE
BEARDED SNAILS

Guam, the westernmost of all United States territories, is an unusual island, though not so unusual as it was sometimes reputed to be during the Second World War. Then American soldiers diligently spread, and occasionally believed, a rumor that the island consisted of a broad shelf of soil delicately balanced atop a slender underwater pinnacle, and that under the edges of the shelf Japanese submarines skulked in cozy safety. Such fantasies aside, the war brought Guam two bonafide distinctions. First, the island, though it is only thirty-two miles long and from four to ten miles wide, became the biggest American possession ever to be conquered by the Japanese. Second, though none of its modest expanse of two hundred and nine square miles ever sheltered any subs, its tangled jungle topside did shelter, for sixteen years, until May, 1960, two Japanese soldiers who can claim, for whatever it may be worth, to have surrendered last of all the millions of participants in the Second World War. Two years after *that*, a conceivably Japanese male, fortyish, was shot and killed on Guam, but his origins are as yet undetermined. So, pending further developments in his case, and until or unless other live claim-

ants turn up, the pair who surrendered in 1960, Masashi
Ito and Bunzo Minagawa, are the kings of the *zanryūsha*,
or stragglers, as this exceedingly hardy species—some of
whom never knew the war had ended and some of whom,
out of fear of death or torture, hid out anyway—has become known in Japan over the years since V-J Day, during which time surprising numbers of such veterans have
returned from far-scattered hideouts on Pacific islands.
And inasmuch as Ito held out two days longer than
Minagawa, he could, if he wished, proclaim himself the
straggliest straggler of them all.

The most southerly of the Mariana Islands, Guam
is an isolated spot. It is more than fifteen hundred miles
east of Manila and just about the same distance southeast
of Tokyo and is the largest land mass in the enormous
expanse of ocean between Hawaii and the Philippines.
It first came to the attention of the Western world in
1521, when Magellan stopped by. The name its oldest
settlers, natives called Chamorros, used for it—and continue to use—was Guahan. The Marianas were claimed
by the Spanish, who named them in honor of Maria
Anna of Austria, the wife of King Philip IV of Spain,
and who established a mission on Guam in 1668. The
Chamorros are still much in evidence, and their language
is still much heard, but other cultures, imported chiefly
from Hawaii and the Philippines, have fused with theirs.
(Filipinos love cockfights, and on Guam cockfighting,
though frowned upon in most areas under the wingspread
of the American eagle, is a legal sport.) Guam has no
industry to speak of and doesn't produce enough food
to sustain its indigenes, who are called Guamanians and

number forty-one thousand. But while nearly everything
the island needs has to be imported from California, six
thousand miles away, Guamanians get along fine. They
are merry and hospitable people, occupying nineteen villages, and each village has at least one bang-up fiesta a
year. On festival days, a stranger may walk into any home
and be warmly received and regaled. Toward the Japanese, however, Guamanians have been inclined since the
war to be a bit less cordial, whatever the day. During the
Japanese control of the island, the occupiers habitually
addressed the Guamanians by the English word "company," intending it to be construed as something close
to "companion." To the occupied, however, the word
had intolerable connotations of both superiority and con-
descension. In Guam these days, to be addressed as
"company" is not considered complimentary.

Guam's climate is so mild—the temperature fluctuates
in a narrow range between seventy and ninety—that much
of the island is covered all year round with dense foliage,
capable of affording excellent concealment to anyone
who wants to hide in it. In 1961, it took a search party
two days to find a couple of women who, with no inten-
tion whatever of hiding, had simply lost their bearings
just outside the capital, Agaña, in what the residents
sometimes call the boondocks. The island is dotted with
caves, some of them big enough to shelter five hundred
men at once. There are mosquitoes on Guam, but there
is no malaria. Wild fruits and vegetables abound. Deer
range the forests, and near the coast shrimp and crab
are plentiful. The surrounding waters are so richly stocked
that Guamanians like to say you can catch fish with your

bare hands if you aren't too tired to bend over. Bounteous as nature has been to Guam, however, Ito and Minagawa were succored no more by the coconuts, breadfruit, papayas, and sweet potatoes that were theirs more or less for the plucking than they were by the prodigality of the American armed forces, which habitually throw away items that would sustain less splendidly endowed outfits in style. Most of the possessions the two Japanese had when they were nabbed had been picked up in an American dump.

Guam came into American hands at the start of the Spanish-American War, when it was seized by the United States Navy, and the Navy has maintained a tight grip on the place almost ever since. (Visitors to the island are apt to be momentarily surprised when they hear that near Agaña the surf is curbed by something called a Glass Breakwater; it is named, they soon learn, after Captain Henry Glass, U.S.N., commander of the U.S.S. Charleston, which subdued the island on June 20, 1898.) Today, although the Air Force has a strategic-bombing base on Guam, the island is still primarily admirals' country, and the military orders that count emanate from Nimitz Hill, where the resident admiral has his headquarters. From 1898 on, the Navy's control of Guam was unchallenged—except, of course, by Japan—until, in 1950, Congress made the island a full-fledged territory with its own civilian governor, appointed by the President and responsible to the Secretary of the Interior. The governor has some peculiar prerogatives—no one else on Guam may import fireworks, for instance—but the

Navy has the bigger guns, the Navy furnishes the whole island with fresh water, and the Navy, which constructed all of Guam's roads, takes care of a large percentage of of them. The Navy's roads are strikingly better than the ones it has turned over to the civilian government, and some of those responsible for the latter resent the Navy's habit of putting up signs at its jurisdictional limits, just before roads turn bumpy, that read, "Navy Maintenance Ends, GovGuam Maintenance Begins."

Since 1950, there has been persistent, if low-pitched, disagreement between the Navy and a good many of the Guamanians about the island's destiny. The first civilian governor expressed the hope that Guam might someday become another Hong Kong, and quite a few local businessmen began enthusiastically dreaming this free-port dream. Others, however, observed that anybody who had the resources and stamina to get to Guam might as well continue to the real Hong Kong. In any event, the Navy has frowned on all moves to open up the island, which it has tended to look upon as a ship—and, what's more, a ship that was not to be overcrowded except during emergencies, at which time it could be converted into a troopship. Until the end of 1961, when long-standing Navy restrictions were lifted, it was impossible for anyone, of whatever nationality, to set foot on Guam without special Navy sanction, and the Navy did not customarily sanction tourists. The airlines serving Guam had— and continued to have—no landing facilities other than the Naval Air Base, and the penalty for debarking a passenger without a Navy clearance was a thousand-dollar fine. (The only hotel, with the exception of a motel that

sprang up in 1961, is a ramshackle quonset-hut establishment, and its patrons are all too noisily reminded who
runs the show; the establishment lies directly beneath
the normal flight path of planes leaving the Navy airfield, a few hundred yards away.) It was the firm inten-
tion of the Navy to keep everybody off the island who
had no business on it. By being strict about who got in,
the Navy felt it could be somewhat more relaxed than
it might otherwise be in its vigilance over those present.
Local Navy regulations for a time forbade travellers who
passed through Guam to take any photographs on, or
even within sight of, the island. But aboard the palm-
fringed ship of Guam, the rule was not severely enforced.
In 1961, an American salesman who passes through
regularly to traffic with Navy Exchange buyers was riding
along the crest of Nimitz Hill with a highly placed naval
officer. They drove by two men in civilian clothes who
were fiddling with a tripod, on which perched a camera
focussed on the harbor of Agaña. "Be sure to mark your
films 'Confidential'!" the officer called out gaily as he
wheeled past them. His companion muttered something
to the effect that he guessed the photographic pair must
be fellow-officers in mufti. "Never saw them before in
my life," said the Navy man, continuing serenely down
the hill.

Some thirty thousand service personnel are stationed
on Guam today, but only four hundred were there on
December 10, 1941, and these could merely offer token
resistance to the five thousand Japanese who swept
ashore that day. A few Navy men chose to flee into the
jungle rather than surrender, and one of them, a com-

municationman named George R. Tweed, managed to
stay under cover for two and a half years, until the
Japanese on Guam had been crushed. He emerged to be
hailed as a hero; the Secretary of the Navy personally
pinned a medal on him, and his as-told-to memoirs were
swiftly published under the title of "Robinson Crusoe,
U.S.N." But though Tweed was the first straggler on
Guam, and the only American one—aside from some
Americans in the Philippines who joined the guerrillas
there, he may have been the only one anywhere—his
glitter did not long remain untarnished. Quite a few
Guamanians had been tortured or killed by the Japanese
for helping him, and among those killed was a priest,
who, according to Tweed's book, had incurred his fate
in part by blabbing confidences told to him in the con-
fessional. Guam is ninety-eight per cent Catholic, and
Tweed's accusation against the priest caused a good deal
of indignation. So did the revelations of some of the
natives who had befriended him, and who complained
that his demands on them and his casual behavior when
he should have been overcautious to avoid exposure and
protect his protectors were unworthy of a hero. All things
considered, Guam now wishes that it had never heard of
this particular Crusoe.

It became evident to the Japanese early in 1944 that
the United States planned to retake Guam, and they decided to make a fight for the base. They had, since 1941,
reduced their garrison to a size almost as small as that of
the force they had displaced, but in the first six months
of 1944 they moved twenty thousand combat troops onto
the island. Twenty thousand was not enough. An Ameri-

can amphibious corps made up mostly of Marines landed on July 21st, which Guamanians have gratefully celebrated ever since as Liberation Day, and on August 10th Guam was pronounced once more secure for the United States.

As the Japanese units on the island began to fall apart, some of their surviving members, in strict adherence to their Bushido code, committed hara-kiri, and others took off into the boondocks. Injuries, illness, and hunger steadily reduced the numbers of these fugitives, but enough of them remained alive to constitute a nuisance—indeed, since many were armed, a menace. In November of 1944, a small, mobile, jungle-wise posse called the Guam Combat Patrol was organized. Its mission was simple: Get the stragglers, dead or alive. The patrol enjoyed no formal military status, but it was outfitted with American Army uniforms and armed with submachine guns, automatic rifles, carbines, pistols, and hand grenades. Composed of fifteen Guamanians, led by a staff sergeant of the Guam police named Juan Aguon, who later became a lieutenant, the patrol roamed the wilds almost every day for a year and a half; at the end of that time Police Headquarters, deciding that unhidden friendly servicemen were beginning to pose more of a threat to law and order than hidden alien ex-servicemen, converted it into a riot squad.

Acting on tips from farmers whose crops or livestock had been pilfered, or who had seen traces of human habitation in areas not normally populated, the patrol tracked down Japanese the length and breadth of Guam. It caught some picking coconuts, others washing clothes, still others playing cards. For the most part, it went in unannounced, with guns blazing, and in all its sorties it bagged only five live Japanese. It killed a hundred and seventeen stragglers, and, in addition, was credited with twenty probables. The patrol itself suffered only two fatalities: one member died of injuries suffered from a fall into a ravine, and another was shot by a Japanese. That happened on the only occasion that Aguon's men invited some surrounded stragglers to give up peaceably. (Once, a wounded Japanese begged the patrol to shoot him again and put him out of his misery; Aguon's subsequent written report noted tersely, "His request was granted.")

Despite the thoroughness of the Combat Patrol—all of its members were ultimately decorated by the United States —nobody on Guam doubted that some Japanese must have escaped Aguon's mop-up. During the next few years, the existence of such strays was periodically made manifest. In April, 1948, a Japanese, who, unlike most of his straggling compatriots, either on Guam or elsewhere, had finally concluded that the war was over and he could safely surrender, stepped out onto a road and waved an old copy of an American magazine at two American military policemen cruising in a jeep. When the M.P.s halted, the Japanese bowed deeply, showed them a photograph in the magazine of the Emperor Hirohito being escorted around Tokyo by American M.P.s, and climbed aboard their vehicle.

Eleven months later, some Guamanian hunters espied two Japanese near Yigo, an inland village in the north-eastern part of the island. The hunters killed one strag-gler; the other got away. A year after that, some American soldiers briefly broke out of a military-police stockade, and on being taken back into custody, they reported that near Tumon Bay, on the northwest coast, they'd seen six Japanese. Being on the lam themselves, they had made no effort to detain the stragglers. In December, 1950, two Guamanian young men were brutally murdered outside Talofofo, a southeastern village. There was no evidence that Japanese had done the wicked deed, but the word went out that stragglers were responsible, and patrols were dispatched to see if any could be found. None were. By that time, the war had been over for five years, and it was becoming hard to tell a straggler from a phantom. At a Navy ammunition magazine outside Agaña, the old hands regularly teased recruits by ad-juring them not to be unduly rattled if, when they were on sentry duty, a Japanese straggler should slip up behind them at two or three o'clock in the morning and scream into their ears. You could never for the life of you hear the little devil approach, the oldtimers would say, and by the time you were sufficiently recovered from the sound of his horrible, homesick screech to swing around, he'd have vanished into the underbrush. As a result of this warning, a jittery recruit would now and then spin through a starless night like a dervish.

The straggler situation on Guam remained un-changed until September 25, 1951. Early that morning, two Guamanian fishermen walking along the beach at Anao Point, a couple of miles from the Andersen Air Force Base, in the northern part of the island, came upon four stragglers asleep on the sand. Aroused, three of them fled, but the fishermen hauled in the fourth. He was Taira Koshin, a thirty-eight-year-old native of Okinawa who had come to Guam eight years before as a civilian employee of a Japanese Navy weather outfit. His beliefs marked him as a singular straggler. He was convinced that the Japanese had lost the war, yet he had not given up hope of being rescued; the Germans were still in contention, he was sure, and sooner or later *they* would save him.

The morning after Koshin's apprehension, the United States Navy and the Guam police mustered a hundred-man force to try and round up his mates. One group of searchers took the Okinawan aboard a self-propelled barge and chugged up toward Anao Point, where Koshin announced in Japanese over a loudspeaker that anyone who happened to hear him would be surprised to learn, as he had learned in the last twenty-four hours, that the war was over on all fronts, and that Japan and the United States were friends. Then Koshin, accompanied by a Naval Intelligence agent and a Guamanian police detective who understood Japanese, rowed ashore in a rubber boat. He led the party up a two-hundred-foot cliff to a well-concealed cave, inside which were four stragglers. Koshin approached the entrance alone, told the men within that the Emperor was alive and well, and advised them to surrender. One of them asked if they should come out armed. (It later developed that they had three bayonets, two razor-sharp G.I. kitchen knives, and a pair of chopsticks.) The detective shouted his assurance that they wouldn't be harmed and, abandoning their weapons, they emerged. One of them, Koshu Yanagi, was a thirty-four-year-old Korean civilian who had been a construction worker for the Japanese; he was clad in a loincloth. The three others, all Japanese, were in ragged American Army uniforms. They were Saburo Akamine, forty-one; Yoshiro Takahashi, thirty-one; and Kihachiro Funaba, thirty. Takahashi had been a radio operator, and Akamine and Funaba airplane mechanics. Before climbing into the rubber boat to ride out to the waiting barge, all four meticulously bathed themselves in the ocean.

The five men told the authorities that they had stayed deep in the jungle from 1944 to 1948, and then had moved to the coast and the caves that pock the seaside cliffs. It was their practice to remain under cover all day and venture forth after dark to gather food, and do calisthenics on the sand. (The night before Koshin was nabbed, they had exercised so strenuously that four of them had decided to take a snooze, and they had overslept.) They had been chased so often by the Guam Combat Patrol and other armed bands that they had become almost obsessively cautious. They always moved in single file. The man in the lead never took a step without first scrutinizing the ground ahead; the last man obliterated their tracks. They tried never to break a twig in an unnatural fashion, or trample down a patch of grass, or displace a stone. They never followed the same route twice. When they picked fruit, they never stripped a tree bare, lest this pique someone's curiosity. During their travels, they conversed in whispers. If any of them happened to mislay a conceivably telltale implement, all five of them always hunted for it until they found it.

Whenever they cooked, they buried their ashes or scattered them in the sea.

On the beach, one memorable moonlit night in August, 1949, the five stragglers had dimly perceived four men approaching them. As the quartet warily drew near, the five tense men could discern that although the newcomers had on American uniforms, they were quite short, and were wearing sandals. A moment later, it was apparent that they were Japanese. There were fervent embraces; it was the first time the members of either group had seen any fellow-countrymen for four harrowing years. The nine held an impromptu feast, and resolved to band together. But in unity there proved to be little strength. The seacoast men were astonished at the life that their brethren, who were making a foray from the interior, confessed to having led. The four were jungle drifters, it seemed—constantly aprowl, and, what was worse, terribly careless. The coastal quintet had, in fact, often come upon oddly damaged coconut trees, and had wondered who had ripped the bark off them. Now it developed that it had been their jungle-dwelling compatriots. Regardless of the differing attitudes of the two groups, it soon became apparent to all that nine men could not hope to live together and avoid detection. So they decided to split up again, and to reconvene once every summer. Funaba went off to spend a month with the jungle contingent and find out all the areas they frequented, so that in the future he could serve as liaison man.

When the five seacoast stragglers were apprehended in that September of 1951, three of the four men in the jungle group were still alive. What happened to the fourth is uncertain. At any rate, the surviving trio had by then moved to the coast, too—to a cave at Pati Point, at the eastern end of Guam and about three miles from Anao Point. The three men had heard Koshin broadcast from the barge, and one of them, a thirty-one-year-old Hokkaido man named Keiichi Kindachi, who had been a civilian cook for a meteorological unit during the war, was sufficiently impressed to come out into the open and seek the source of the bewildering news that the war had ended. He walked the beach in vain that day, so the next day he tried a different tack. At seven o'clock in the morning, the Filipino driver of a military bus taking Air Force employees to work was flabbergasted to come upon a Japanese, naked except for a loincloth, standing in the middle of the road, his arms upraised. It was Kindachi. He had been away from civilization so long that he may have thought the bus was a house, for before he would get aboard he ceremoniously removed his sandals. The bus driver, ignoring the stops on his route, hightailed it for the nearest Provost Marshal's office. The following day, after Kindachi had been interrogated, another search got under way. Kindachi led a party to his cliff dwelling. Nobody was home, but he left a reassuring note for his friends—Seisaku Kitamura and Hazuo Hoshi. On finding Kindachi's note, the pair walked toward a rendezvous he had specified, and shortly before noon on September 28th a sentry at the Andersen base spotted them. Both men had dressed themselves for the occasion in white mess jackets, which they had presumably swiped from an unsecured Navy wash.

The apprehension of these eight men—who, after some cursory police interrogation about the 1950 murders, were packed off to Japan—represented the biggest week's haul of live Guam stragglers since the end of the war, and it spurred renewed activity all over the island. Patrols combed Guam throughout 1952, egged on by a report that two sailors idling on a cliff at Orote, on the western shore, had seen a fierce-looking Japanese brandishing a carbine, and by another report that some civilian picnickers on a beach at Talofofo, on the other side of the island, had seen a harmless-looking Japanese fishing in a cove. No stragglers were found.

Early in 1953, the Japanese government was allowed to send a party to Guam to collect the bones of its troops who had died there and take them home for burial. These emissaries heard so much talk on the island about stragglers who were still theoretically at large there that, after their return to Japan, they suggested that somebody do something more about getting the expatriates home. So presently the Japanese government shipped a batch of leaflets to Guam, with the request that they be strewn around at spots where cave dwellers or cliff scalers might find them. These were addressed to "the Japanese stragglers on Guam" and were signed by a former lieutenant colonel, Touru Itagaki, who, as head of the Repatriation Section of the Repatriation Aid Bureau of the Ministry of Health and Welfare, had since the end of the war been, and still is, the Japanese individual most intimately concerned with stragglers. Itagaki's communication told how the war had ended and how other stragglers had been rescued, and went on:

This long dark age of yours is coming to an end. Happiness and joy lie ahead of you. . . . This is not a trick, or a dream. It is true and real. . . . Here is an example. Eight men who were in Guam, just as you are now, surrendered in September, 1951, to the U.S. armed forces there. After being well treated there, all of them came home here, in high spirits, and have been enjoying life in their own country with their families. If you cannot believe this, please write a letter. You can use the envelope and paper we are enclosing. We promise to deliver your letter to your family, get an answer, and bring it back to this same spot.

Soon after these words of cheer were disseminated, a jungle patrol on Guam came upon a piece of deerhorn carved into a *hanko*—the personal seal used by most Japanese in lieu of a signature. Three more deerhorn seals were found nearby. The names on the four seals were Akachi, Ito, Kobayashi, and Yorita. This intelligence was transmitted to Tokyo, and the Repatriation Section at once began to check the names against available government records of soldiers who had been on Guam and were unaccounted for. Itagaki came up with two Akachis, two Itos, four Kobayashis, and three Yoritas. The families of all eleven men were asked to compose messages to their missing kin. These were printed up and, that August, were placed in eight spots on Guam.

The sister of Issaki Ito, a man whose fate is still unknown, wrote from her village of Koseki:

A hot summer with a beating sun has come. I am Tatsuji. You can't imagine how much I've been missing you. Our mother is fine. Haruji's grown up to be a nice young man, and his younger brother Akio is now big enough to beat up Haruji. Why don't you come back? . . . You just go out to a village and tell the people you are a Japanese and want to come back home. That is all you have to do. . . . We have a new junior high school now in Koseki. The farming school at Kunado has been turned into a senior high school. . . . A bus is running now from Sannomiya-Shihashi to Kunado station by way of Shibakusa, and another bus has started to run from Tokiwa station to Moto-su via Koseki. . . . Come back immediately, dear brother. If you go to the police or to the American forces, they'll send you home on a ship, right away. There'll be no danger. Mother asked me to give you her best wishes. . . .

The father of Masashi Ito wrote from his village of Shimobe:

The rainy season has gone now. The weather is getting real hot, and we are really busy on the farm. The other day, an official in the town office came and told us that several men of the Kofu Regiment might still be alive, and he also said a man named Ito is among them. I want you to be Masashi, and to come out right away. That is why I am writing this letter. I am writing this in a great hurry. You are the only one in this village who didn't come back. Your mother never stops talking about you. Your grandmother died the year before last, from worrying about you. Kimiko [Ito's sister] is waiting for you, still unmarried. Everything is better after the war. Mr. Kazushi Akaji bought a small truck and is driving around in it. You come back. All you have to do is walk out of the jungle with a white flag, I hear. They won't kill you, or put you in jail, they say. Come back as soon as possible. I'll be waiting.

Masashi Ito never saw that letter. Nor did he see complementary messages, signed "Japanese Government," that implored him to look for and read his personal mail. "Maybe you cannot make up your mind, worrying about things out in the jungle," one of these missives said. "There's no danger. We promise you. There are no armed forces now in Japan, and, of course, no military penal code. You'll never be put on trial. Come on out as soon as possible. In a month, you'll be spending wonderful days with your family and friends at your home, surrounded by the good old mountains and rivers. Stop worrying and make up your mind."

Back in April, Ito had seen the Repatriation Section's first letter, and he had then made up his mind—almost. Using the pencil and paper his government had furnished, he wrote a note soliciting further contact. Just in case somebody was pulling a fast one, though, he circumspectly signed his note "Bunya Aihara"—the name of one of his closest friends, who had enlisted with him at Kofu eleven years earlier, had sailed with him to Guam, and had been fatally injured in an air raid a week before the island was retaken by the Americans. But the two men then in hiding with Ito, Bunzo Minagawa and Tetsuo Unno, were even more suspicious than he was. Some current Tokyo newspapers had been distributed on Guam along with the letters to the stragglers, and in one of them the three men had read that the price of bean cake was ten yen a serving. The news columns of the papers seemed plausible enough, but ten yen for bean cake was ludicrous. A private soldier's monthly pay was twenty yen, or had been the last time they'd had anything to do with money. The men on Guam did not know, of course, to what extent postwar inflation had hit Japan. Minagawa and Unno were convinced that any newspaper that cited so preposterous a price for bean cake must be a phony. Moreover, they told Ito, this whole business of claiming that the war was over and suggesting an exchange of letters was probably a ruse to get them to disclose their whereabouts. Ito was swayed by the majority view, and tore up his reply. He never laid eyes on another invitation to get in touch with anybody. He and Minagawa were to hold out for seven more years in the jungle, and during that time his waiting father died. So did Unno.

Encouraged by the discovery of the seals (all of them had been whittled by Ito, who came from a region of *hanko*-makers, whose lifelong hobby had been carving, and who had placed on the three seals other than his own the surnames of old acquaintances), the Japanese government was eager to send a search party to Guam. The American Navy opposed the scheme; as far as it was concerned, there were already too many aliens without security clearances wandering around its precincts. Navy and GovGuam officials agreed, however, to undertake a new search of their own, and Itagaki's office in Tokyo furnished them with additional hortatory literature. In late November, 1953, something that the Navy felt it had to christen Operation Straggler was launched. Packages were left in caves, posters were nailed to trees, and a Navy plane dropped fifteen thousand leaflets. The searchers concentrated on southern Guam; village officials in that area were asked to insure safe conduct for any Japanese who heeded the call, while parish priests preached sermons counselling restraint and charity toward the ex-enemy. Operation Straggler was a fizzle. One patrol found a human skull, a second found what seemed to be a lookout platform in a coconut tree, and a third found a snail so recently squashed by someone's foot that it was still alive. And that was all.

Nearly four years passed before Guam once more got stirred up about stragglers. On September 14, 1957, some off-duty Marines, hiking in the vicinity of the Navy ammunition magazine, came upon a camp site, complete with cooking gear and hand tools. They reported their discovery to Naval Intelligence, and Intelligence, alarmed at the notion that anyone had been nosing around the edges of the island's principal cache of ammunition, at once whipped up an intensive investigation. Now *on*-duty Marines patrolled the region. They found the ashes of a fire; a pile of breadfruit, shrimp, and coconuts; some sleeping pads made of logs and palm fronds; a pair of *tabi*, or Japanese slit-toed socks; and, hanging from a tree limb, some chopsticks and a toothbrush, the latter bearing a Japanese Navy emblem. On a riverbank they found a hat. In a cave they found four hack-saw blades, three files, a saw, two pot holders, three rounds of rifle ammunition, a pestle, a jar of oil, some cooking pots, and two pieces of wood tied together with wire. This last object Naval Intelligence nervously decided was a garrote. The searchers also found a small, crude two-wheeled wooden cart, which Intelligence even more nervously deduced could have been used to trundle a fifty-gallon drum of gasoline. (Ito had fashioned the cart, but not to haul anything explosive. He merely wanted to be able to transport some gear he'd otherwise have had to tote on his back to a new camp site. Both he and Minagawa were weary and backsore; Minagawa has since described his stooped and straggling self at the time as " a snail with a beard." Ito had not quite finished his cart, and was put out, on returning to the place where he'd left it, to find that someone had stolen it.)

In another cave, the Marines found a glass bottle etched with an encircled Japanese character, which, a local Japanese scholar surmised, stood for "Ito." (Ito had used the bottle to store salt in.) The Navy concluded that all this stuff belonged either to stragglers or to espionage agents. Exploring the latter possibility, the Navy determined to ascertain what spies could have seen; it sent photographers to the summits of the hills closest to the caves, had them take pictures of the ammunition depot, and glumly studied the results, which were quite revealing. However, when the Guam *Daily News* got wind of all this bustling in the boondocks and asked the Navy what was going on, the Navy replied merely that it seemed to have uncovered a poachers' lair.

A few months after the Marines had gathered in all their booty, a woman playing out of the rough at the Windward Hills Golf and Country Club, a couple of miles east of the Navy magazine and eight miles from Agaña, was distracted in the midst of a backswing by a brief but clear glimpse of a scrawny, raggedly dressed, long-haired person who darted away. She flubbed the shot. Later, to excuse her poor score on that particular hole, she told her partner that some exasperating native woman had startled her, but then she bemusedly recalled that her distracter had had a beard. The Navy, to which the incident was duly reported, did nothing this time— conceivably, it has been suggested, because by then the Navy had concluded it did not want to find any more stragglers. If it had found one, it would have had to send him to Japan, and what properly security-conscious headquarters staff would wish to turn loose an un- screened individual who had spent a dozen years acquir- ing a possibly inch-by-inch knowledge of a restricted area? Better to leave him out there—so the thinking may have run— and let him rot.

On May 21, 1960, exactly fifteen years and ten months after the liberation of Guam, Vicente Manibusan and Clemente Santos, two Guamanians from Talofofo, the village nearest the golf course, rose at dawn to go out and check some traps they'd set for coconut crabs, which are large and meaty land crabs, sometimes weigh- ing as much as twenty pounds, that live on fruit and are especially partial to coconuts. The two men were walking through the underbrush when, a hundred yards ahead of them, they saw a long-haired, bewhiskered Japanese strolling along, with a sack in his hand. It was Minagawa, who had started out that day with the idea of stealing a chicken, but, having been put off by some noisy roosters, had decided to settle instead for a bag of breadfruit. While Santos and Manibusan watched covertly, the Japanese scrambled thirty feet up the trunk of a bread- fruit tree. The Guamanians closed in on him, and Manibusan, standing directly beneath him, shouted "Company!" Minagawa let out a strangled "Agh!," fell from the tree, sprang up, and began running. A couple of hundred feet away, Manibusan caught up with him and grabbed his shirt. Breaking loose, Minagawa lunged for a knife at the Guamanian's belt. Santos had reached them by then, and he grasped the straggler's hand. As Minagawa fought to get clear, the Guamanians punched him in the head and finally subdued him. (Minagawa was unarmed; in two pouches fastened to his belt, he was carrying a dirty bandage and a small wooden Buddha.) Tying his arms behind his back with his belt, the Guamanians marched him to the Talofofo-Agaña highway, where they figured they could get a lift to the nearest police station. The drivers of the first three cars they flagged took an appraising look at the unkempt, filthy, glaring Japanese and drove hastily on. Finally, a friend of the Guamanians' happened by and gave them and their prisoner a hitch.

Minagawa was soon at Agaña police headquarters, where, upon being offered some coffee and doughnuts, he spurned them as though they were poison. A Japanese-speaking detective questioned him, but got little more out of him than his name. Minagawa was too scared to talk; he believed he had fallen into the hands of the enemy, and would be tortured or killed at any minute. The Guam police are part of the island's Division of Public Safety, and its then director, a retired Marine Corps brigadier general named Jesse S. Cook, was shortly in perplexed consultation about the Japanese with representatives of the United States Attorney's office, the Immigration Department, GovGuam, and the Navy. To

whom did this unexpected prize belong? According to the
1950 Act of Congress relating to the territory, natives of
Guam as of that date were automatically American citi-
zens. Then was this fellow, who had been on the island
for goodness knows how long and refused to divulge his
origins, technically an American? (Nobody had thought
to raise this point when the 1951 stragglers were caught
and hustled back to Japan.) If he was an alien, which
seemed much more logical, did he have to be prosecuted
for having violated the McCarran Act of 1950, which
decreed that all non-citizens residing on United States
soil must thereafter register at a federal office every
January? Whatever Minagawa was, could he or should
he be booked on some local charge—trespassing, poach-
ing, theft, murder, lack of a Navy clearance? And how
long *had* he been around, anyway? He had obviously not
seen a barber for quite some time, but his hands and
feet were not notably calloused. Could he, by any chance,
be some sort of a spy who had been landed on Guam by
submarine? If so, the Navy didn't want him in the
custody of the local police, who didn't have high enough
security clearances to handle that sort of top-level in-
trigue. It was at last agreed that the fellow would be clas-
sified as an alien without proper credentials and turned
over to Immigration, but that since Immigration had no
facilities for keeping him under surveillance, he would be
placed in the Naval Hospital in Agaña. Naval Intelligence
transported him there, gave him a shave and a haircut,
and locked him up in the neuropsychiatric ward. (Immigration, which wanted to keep its records straight, was
ultimately satisfied when Minagawa—and in his turn Ito,

too—signed an affidavit stating, in first-rate bureaucratic gibberish, "At the time of entry I had no documents permitting my entry on Guam.")

The Navy began looking around for an interpreter who could pry something out of its uncommunicative captive, and found a likely prospect in the person of Edward G. Tsutsui, a Hawaiian-born Nisei who was employed as a packer and crater in its own supply depot. At first, Tsutsui got nowhere. Minagawa was not only uncommunicative but implacably suspicious. When he was told to take a bath, he thought this was some sort of pre-execution cleansing ritual. When he was pricked for a blood specimen, he thought he was being drugged. When anyone at the hospital tried to be nice to him, he thought it was a ruse. He wouldn't believe anything Tsutsui told him. Minagawa did tell the Nisei the truth about who he was and how long he'd been on Guam. He insisted, though, that he'd been living alone. He has since explained that he expected to be killed, and he didn't want to expose Ito to the same sorry fate. Then, after almost forty-eight hours of interrogation, he confessed that he had had a companion, who was still at liberty. "When they caught me, I thought maybe they'd wait two or three days before they killed me, and that if I kept quiet about Ito for that long, it would give him time to get away to a spot we'd picked to move to in case we got in trouble," Minagawa said recently.

As soon as the Navy learned about Ito, it sallied forth to get him, without bothering to notify the civil authorities, in whose jurisdictional area, as it happened, the roundup was conducted. Minagawa was put aboard a helicopter with Tsutsui and a Naval Intelligence man, and two additional Intelligence agents boarded a second copter. (The agents were armed, and afterward the civil authorities could not resist pointing out that if a Navy man had shot Ito in non-Navy territory, he could have been charged with homicide.) The party landed near the place where Minagawa had been caught, and he, feeling confident that Ito had by then realized what was up and had scurried elsewhere, led them to the shelter Ito and he had been occupying. The shelter was abandoned, and the Navy men asked Minagawa where they ought to look next. The Japanese shrugged. "Find out for yourself," he said.

The shelter was situated near the foot of a hill, and two of the Intelligence agents now began working their way toward the hilltop. En route, they unknowingly passed Ito, who was crouching halfway up the slope. Two days earlier, he had gone to look for Minagawa and had found his companion's empty sack near the breadfruit tree. "I was sure Minagawa had been captured," he says, "and I made up my mind to give myself up." Whatever might befall him, he had reasoned, could be no worse than a future of utter solitude. He had seen the helicopters approaching, and had guessed he was their quarry. Minagawa, though, didn't know what was in Ito's mind, and at the foot of the hill he began yelling, "Ito-san! Ito-san!" The agents thought he was calling for Ito to come out, but Minagawa, who in the years gone by had never conversed with Ito except in hushed tones, says he was shouting his lustiest in the hope that Ito would be warned to make a dash for it. Ito didn't hear Minagawa at all. By

then, he was walking up the hill, waving a piece of cloth
in lieu of a flag of truce, and when he got to the top he
walked right into the arms of the two agents there.

Back at the hospital, both men had physical exami-
nations, and both were pronounced fit. Ito had a slight
rash on his face and upper body, and some muscle sore-
ness. Minagawa's worst ailment was a laceration he'd
suffered when the Guamanian crab trappers bashed him
on the ear. Tsutsui didn't have much better luck in
interrogating the two men together than he'd had with
Minagawa alone. No matter how many times, and in how
many ways, the Nisei tried to reassure them, they reacted with stony skepticism. At night, when they were
left by themselves, they seriously discussed committing
suicide. Minagawa thought maybe he could slash himself with a piece of bedspring. As for Ito, the following
morning he forthrightly asked Tsutsui to fetch him a
knife or a gun. Tsutsui, still seeking some means of getting through to the men, brought them some Japanese
magazines, full of words and pictures attesting to the
serenity of their homeland. The stragglers were only
mildly interested until, in one journal, they came upon
a photograph of a Japanese girl embracing an American
soldier. Minagawa flung the magazine down. "It's a lie!"
he said angrily. "First, we do not kiss, and, second, a
Japanese woman would never let herself be kissed by a
Yankee!"

By now, representatives of practically every official
and semi-official agency on Guam were swarming around
Ito and Minagawa. The United States was conducting
its 1960 census, and a conscientious census-taker in

Agaña, determined to count every living soul within his purview, took suitable data from both stragglers. Ito's and Minagawa's names had been stricken, when they were presumed to have died in action, from the population registers that are maintained in Japan's regional prefectures; as a result, the census-taker conferred on them an official existence in the United States that they did not at that moment enjoy in their native land. Concurrently, the perplexed Navy, which had satisfied itself that the two men were legitimate stragglers and harbored no designs on any of its secrets, asked the American Red Cross to do what it could about helping them see the light. The principal Red Cross worker assigned to the Naval Hospital, Miss Mary Jane Dom, cabled her headquarters in Japan suggesting that arrangements be made for the men's families to telephone them. "Unable convince patients that relatives alive and no shame to return home," her cable went. "Also requesting new clothing for travel home." In Tokyo, the Japanese National Red Cross began setting up the phone calls, and at the same time the enterprising *Asahi Shimbun*, Japan's biggest paper, got permission from the United States Navy for one of its reporters, Tsugio Kato, to fly to Guam.

On May 26th, before the Red Cross could get its connections made, Minagawa's married older sister, Tsuru Nakabayashi, who had read stories about the stragglers in Japanese newspapers, put through a call on her own. Minagawa could not hear her well, and did not recognize her voice. After some fruitless shouting, he slammed the phone down in disgust. The *Asahi* man reached Guam that night. He brought along a letter to

Ito from *his* sister, Kimiko, and a bundle of presents she'd hastily wrapped—a package of raisins, some seaweed cookies, and a few family snapshots. Ito began to wonder if maybe Tsutsui hadn't been on the level after all, but he was still far from completely won over. Minagawa remained obdurate.

The next day, May 27th, the Red Cross calls came through.

"Masashi, this is your sister Kimiko," Ito heard. "Yes —Kimiko. Can you hear me? . . . Are you sure you can hear me? . . . I'm so glad. I was certain you were dead. I hadn't the faintest idea you were alive. How are you? . . . Well, look, the war ended fifteen years ago. Do you understand?"

Ito said he did.

"Please come back," she went on. "Mother will be here. . . . Yes, Mother will be here. . . . Yes, she is well. Please come home. Saturday night, we will go to our home together. . . . We can walk in the fields again, just as when we were children."

Then it was Minagawa's turn.

"Is this Bunzo?"

"Who are you?"

"This is your sister, Tsuru. Aren't you Bunzo?"

"Yes, this is Bunzo. Who are you? . . . Who? . . . What part of Niigata Prefecture are you from? . . . How much land do we own? . . . What is the name of the third daughter of the family that used to live next door to us?"

Mrs. Nakabayashi did her best, but—largely because, in her excitement, she got the extent of the family acreage wrong—she failed to convince her brother that it was ac-

tually she he was talking with. His disbelief was conta-
gious; Ito now thought that he might have been duped,
too. That night, the last of their thousands of nights on
Guam, Tsutsui threw a party for them at his home, with
sukiyaki and beer and whiskey, but in this convivial setting the stragglers remained apathetic and aloof.

The following morning, May 28th, the Navy flew Ito
and Minagawa to Japan. Tsutsui and two Intelligence
agents rode along. As they boarded the plane, Ito grinned
broadly and waved both arms at the bystanders seeing
them off, like a victorious prizefighter—or, perhaps, like a
man putting on a show of bravado before a firing squad.
Minagawa, in more conventional Japanese fashion, bowed
deeply and sombrely, but then, observing Ito's gesture,
he half-heartedly imitated it. The stragglers were wearing
brand new suits. It is customary on Guam, when some
shipwrecked sailor or other hapless person needs clothing, to fit him out in somebody's hand-me-downs. But
American-Japanese relations were strained that week. The
riots that cancelled President Eisenhower's proposed visit
to Tokyo were in full swing, and all hands on Guam decided that it would be politically desirable for the United
States to return its two Japanese in the nattiest shape
possible. Moreover, the Red Cross had notified Miss Dom
she could splurge on a couple of ensembles. It is not easy
to buy a whole suit on Guam. Because of the heat, hardly
anybody ever wears a jacket, and most clothing stores
merely stock pants. But at one shop Miss Dom found a
two-piece tan outfit in Ito's size, at $53.90, and a brown
one, for Minagawa, a relative bargain at $39.95. Each
man also got a new white shirt—to Japanese, a sartorial

symbol of civilian life. The Navy had undertaken to fur-
nish shoes, and in a conference with the Red Cross had
decided that brown would go most agreeably with the
stragglers' costumes. At the last minute, however, there
was a snafu, and the Navy produced black shoes. Miss
Dom was devastated.

Ito and Minagawa couldn't have cared less. Their
thoughts were still separated by a vast gulf of misunder-
standing and mistrust from the thoughts of, for instance,
the editors of the Guam *Daily News*, who in a farewell
editorial to the pair entitled "New World for Two" and
printed on the day of their departure said, "However
bleak the world outside the jungles may be, we're sure
they will not regret that they are out of it, and we hope
they will share in every opportunity to contribute to
world peace and to foster the good relations between
their country and ours." On the plane, the patient
Tsutsui continued to assure the men that they would
soon receive a warm and loving welcome from their
kinsfolk, but they remained preoccupied with thoughts
of doom. Ito later said that he had expected to be pushed
out of the plane into the Pacific. Minagawa expected the
craft to land on some isolated island, where he would
be thrown into a concentration camp for war prisoners.
As they sighted land, Minagawa asked Tsutsui challeng-
ingly, "Where is Mount Fuji?" Because of clouds, that
majestic landmark had not come into view, and all that
the men in the plane could see was some unremarkable
low-lying Japanese soil. Minagawa said it didn't look
like Japan to *him*. The plane alighted at the Tachikawa
Air Base, an American installation on the outskirts of

Tokyo, and as it taxied to a halt it was surrounded by a thousand United States airmen and two hundred Japanese reporters and photographers, among them a delegation of twenty from *Asahi* alone. Ito and Minagawa, blinking, walked down the landing stairs, and the Americans burst into applause. The stragglers were confounded by what their ears heard, but when their eyes took in the swarm of Yankee uniforms, their gloomiest surmise was confirmed: Japan had indeed become a colony in servile thrall to the enemy. It was only when, a few moments later, they were physically clasped in the embraces of tear-streaked relatives that either of them believed everything was finally going to be all right.

2

OH,
WHAT A MISERABLE
LIFE THIS IS!

Masashi Ito and Bunzo Minagawa had similar backgrounds, which differed little from the background of the run-of-the-mill Japanese foot soldier. Both were eldest sons—and, as such, the most privileged offspring—of small-scale farmers. Both were men of only moderate intelligence and no great emotional sensitivity, who had gone through the eighth grade in rural schools and had then taken their places in the family paddy fields. Minagawa, a stocky, jug-eared man, was born on August 22, 1920, in the village of Kurokawa, in Niigata Prefecture, three hundred miles northwest of Tokyo. This is snow country; his mother was killed in an avalanche in 1938. His father died two years afterward, and Minagawa went to live with relatives. Ito was born on March 1, 1921, in Shimobe, in Yamanashi Prefecture, a hundred and fifty miles west of Tokyo. He has had a pronounced stutter since boyhood, and he stands five feet ten inches, which is tall for a Japanese. When he was undergoing the conventionally rigorous recruit training of his country, some of his superiors had to stand on tiptoe to hit him in the face.

Both stragglers were a few months short of twenty-

one when they joined the Army—Minagawa on April 10,
1941, and Ito on January 10, 1942. Like most Japanese
soldiers, they went into service accoutred with a *sennimbari*, a sash of a thousand stitches, and an *omamori*, a
good-luck amulet. Ito also tried to take with him a *yose-
gaki*, a Japanese flag on which his friends had put their
signatures, but the Army, though it was appreciative of
his patriotism, vetoed the banner as excess baggage. Ito
trained in Manchuria, Minagawa in Japan. Neither of
them had experienced any combat when, in the winter of
1944, their outfits were shipped to the Marianas. Both
sailed in a convoy that reached Saipan, northeast of
Guam in that island group, on March 19th. Ito's unit
moved on to Guam two days later; Minagawa got there
on June 5th. By that time, both men held the rank of
heicho, a cut above private first class. During the fighting
on Guam, they, like just about all their comrades-in-arms,
almost at once found their units hopelessly disorganized.
Ito and some of the men in his platoon, for instance,
were ordered up into the hills, then told to prepare for
an all-out attack, and then told it had been called off.
After that, they heard practically nothing from any official quarter, and the combat they engaged in consisted of
little more than a few guerrillalike skirmishes. Both Ito
and Minagawa were officially declared dead in the fall of
1944, after the Japanese had put on a final desperate
banzai attack. This debacle, in which neither man took
part, occurred on September 30th, which was just a few
weeks before the two met for the first time and embarked
on a mutual and well-nigh interminable adventure that
was equally notable for its richness of interdependence

and for its poverty of friendship. "To be honest, we were not the sort of men who in ordinary circumstances would have been good friends," Minagawa asserted afterward. "The only thing we had in common was a determination to live."

It is not always the fittest or the hardiest who survive. Sometimes it is the luckiest. Minagawa, for instance, tried to commit suicide very shortly after the United States retook Guam. When a Guamanian patrol came upon a cave he was hiding in, Minagawa, resolving to be neither shot nor captured, clutched a grenade to his chest and pulled the pin. The grenade was defective. Putting it aside, he hid himself beneath a blanket in a dark corner. The patrol failed to spot him, and passed on to the next cave, gunning down a sizable party of Japanese within it.

Minagawa's first companion in the jungle, with whom he joined forces when the last organized Japanese resistance collapsed, was a former rug salesman named Tokujiro Miyazawa. Foraging in a native village one night, they found a chicken, and were so hungry they ate it raw, on the spot. A couple of days later, they returned to this oasis of relative plenty and espied a fat, alluring calf. As they approached it, it ran toward its mother, who was grazing nearby, and took shelter under her belly. Minagawa dragged the calf out and slashed its throat with a sabre. "The mother was looking at me, crying," he has recalled, somewhat over-imaginatively. "She must have loved that calf. Watching the tears roll down her cheeks, we were deeply sorry for what we'd done, but we had to live." While the cow stared at them reproachfully, they butchered the calf with their sabres, ate some of the meat raw, and wrapped the rest in coconut leaves. Later that night, Minagawa and Miyazawa were lying in a coconut grove, gazing at the moon and whispering about Japan, when two armed men, one wearing an American Navy cap, came within forty feet of them. The pair passed by, and the Japanese moved at once to another area, taking their supply of meat with them.

Minagawa and Miyazawa settled into a cave near the Tokui River, just north of the golf course, and when they had been there only a few days, a haggard Japanese soldier crept up and asked haltingly if he could join them. It was Ito. He had been drifting around aimlessly since, a few hours earlier, he had survived an American ambush that decimated a group of stragglers he'd been travelling with. Minagawa and Miyazawa invited him in. The cave seemed a mite cramped for three men, so they moved along the Tokui, seeking a larger one. During this trek, they came upon two additional parties of stragglers. A lieutenant was leading one of them, and he told the three men not to be disheartened, because before long the Imperial Army would surely come and rescue them all. Although the three were somewhat cheered by this prospect of ultimate deliverance, they struck off on their own again, figuring that it would be imprudent to remain with so large a group. "We felt that we had a better chance of surviving if we tried to be self-sufficient," Minagawa says. "We were sustained by remembering that Heaven helps those who help themselves." Minagawa, a devout Buddhist, is convinced that his faith is what gave him the strength to endure. "Belief is power," he says. In one

jungle cave, he found his small carved Buddha, and thereafter he carried it with him wherever he went, praying to
it every morning and every night. Minagawa takes various
rural Japanese superstitions very seriously. One day, when
the three men were drying their clothes on a big flat rock,
the rock suddenly split in two. Minagawa viewed this as
a dire omen, and insisted that they change their place of
residence pronto. Ito and Miyazawa thought their companion's fears nonsensical, but they agreed to switch hideouts. The trio now took over a cave, halfway up a cliff,
that proved to be better than most; at the top of the cliff
was a native village, and after dark the stragglers could
climb up and help themselves to bananas, potatoes, and
tapioca grown by the resident farmers.

The three men had been in this cave a month before
they became aware, after spotting some unnaturally
broken twigs, that other people—a colony of seven Japanese, it turned out—were living in a hut only five hundred
feet from them. These seven were the remnants of a supply company, and, like most supply troops everywhere,
they had managed to maintain a fairly well-stocked
larder. They had rice and bean paste, for instance—delicacies that Ito, Minagawa, and Miyazawa hadn't tasted
for months. "When we discovered them, we asked them
what their plans were," Minagawa says. "They said they
were going to stay where they were until our Army came
and rescued them. They asked us what our plans were,
and we had to admit we didn't have any."

Returning to their cave, the three men had a long
talk about the future. They concluded that they, too,
should build themselves a comfortable hut and wait for

help. Some five hundred yards from their cave was still another native settlement, an abandoned one. A few of its cluster of houses had tin roofs, and the Japanese decided to take some sheets of tin into the jungle and use them to roof a cabin of their own. Since the sheets were awkward to carry, Ito and Miyazawa were for clearing a trail to expedite the job. Minagawa vehemently dissented. "I told them, 'If you cut down trees, the natives will see this and come after us,'" he says. "'We might as well build a cabin right out in the open.' But they said we couldn't move the tin unless we cut a path. So I said, 'If you stick to that plan, I'm going to have to leave you, because I don't want to die before the Japanese Army comes for me.'"

Ito and Miyazawa went ahead, and Minagawa left them and attached himself to the supply men. By then, three more drifters had joined that group. As the eleven of them were sitting around their hut one morning—Minagawa thinks it was in July of 1945, but it may have been a bit earlier—the Guam Combat Patrol struck. Four Japanese were killed, and one was badly wounded. The rest fled into the brush, and when the patrol gave up looking for them and went away, they got together again and decided to move, in a hurry. The wounded man, who had managed to stagger out of the patrol's surveillance before collapsing, had been blinded and couldn't walk or talk. None of the others had the strength to carry him, so they put some breadfruit within his reach and moved on. The following day, they were attacked again, and dived into a thicket at the base of a hill. From above, a voice began broadcasting to them in Japanese over a public-address system, urging them to surrender and join the speaker in a cup of coffee and some bread and jam. The refreshments sounded tempting, but a murmur of American voices that was also audible over the loudspeaker prompted the stragglers to keep mum.

Minagawa and his companions concluded that there were just too many of them hanging around together for safety, and that they had better divide up. He paired off with Tetsuo Unno, the handsome, smooth-talking son of a farmer in Shizuoka Prefecture, southwest of Tokyo. Between them, Unno and Minagawa had two sabres, two caps, a pair of gloves, and a hand mirror. Minagawa had picked up the mirror somewhere along the way, and he clung to it assiduously. "There was no special reason for it," he said later. "Maybe I wanted to keep reminded that I was I." They were able to add to these possessions when they came upon an American supply dump near the mouth of the Tokui River. Here were some shirts, and mosquito netting, and a whetstone for honing their swords, and some tires from which they could cut sandals. Here, too, were shoes, of the right size, but the men were afraid the heels would leave telltale marks, so they sliced up the leather and from it fashioned scabbards for their sabres.

Minagawa and Unno knew that Ito and Miyazawa were encamped not far away, and after some months Minagawa and his companion paid a call on them. The visitors found their hosts snugly encamped in a tin-roofed hut, which Minagawa has since described as "gorgeous." However, Ito and Miyazawa had by then cleared so many trails around their abode that Minagawa and Unno—who as a rule crawled through bushes in preference to hacking away at them revealingly—were sure their friends would sooner or later be spotted. They were. In December, 1945—about four months after V-J Day—Ito and Miyazawa caught a stray calf and dragged it to their shelter. As they were butchering it, some natives who had followed their trail sneaked up and opened fire. Miyazawa was killed instantly. Ito escaped. A few days later, he sought out Minagawa and Unno and asked if he could move in with them. The three of them remained together for almost eight years, and during that time three, as so often happens, proved to be a crowd.

By mid-1946, the Guam Combat Patrol was slackening its pace, but the backwoods of the island were by no means restful for wandering Japanese. The place was swarming with armed men, and the fact that many of them were gunning for deer rather than for former enemy troops made little difference to the latter. The deer problem stemmed from the days of the Japanese occupation, when the animals had been mowed down for food in exorbitant numbers. Now the American authorities, in the hope that the remaining deer would breed back up to the level of Guam's prewar herd, had instituted a strict conservation program, which forbade hunting in any season. It followed, inevitably, that poachers were aprowl in all seasons. It was a thirty-nine-year-old Guamanian fork-lift operator, trespassing in a Naval area and carrying an unlicensed shotgun, who in the spring of 1962 shot and killed a man he has insisted was a Japanese. The Guamanian was foraging for betel nuts in forbidden territory on April 20th, Good Friday, when, according to his story, a Japanese lurking in the underbrush threw a hatchet at him. The trespasser wounded his assailant, approached him, and tried to talk to him in English, Chamorro, and Japanese. But the wounded man wouldn't reply. Instead, he moved a foot, as if to kick, and the Guamanian shot him dead. Since the aggressor had no business being where he was, he didn't tell anybody what had happened until May 9th. By the time the island authorities went to the scene, wild boars had got there ahead of them. All that was to be found were a few bones, and a single *zori*, a Japanese sandal. The Guamanian had described his victim as short-haired and clean-shaven; a pathologist who examined the bones could say definitely only that the dead man was five feet, one and a half inches tall, of Asiatic origin, and between thirty-five and fifty years old. In Tokyo, Minagawa, asked if he thought the victim could have been a straggler, expressed doubt; the man had been in a region quite near his and Ito's haunts, and he just couldn't believe they wouldn't have come upon *some* trace of his existence. When the fork-lift operator was indicted, for manslaughter, the bill of particulars referred to the slain man merely as "a human being."

While Minagawa and Ito were in the same jungle area, military units on training patrols and other missions also frequented the region. The two stragglers had no idea what lay behind all this pedestrian traffic; they simply knew that they had to be ever on the alert for men roaming around with loaded weapons. (Japanese psychologists have since speculated that an almost all-consuming fear of being assaulted gave the stragglers a kind of social contact—if only at a distance—with other humans that made their isolated life more tolerable than it would have been if they'd had a chance to relax.) In the whole six-teen years Ito and Minagawa hid out, not a single week went by in which they did not glimpse or hear at least one armed band. In 1947, Ito was precariously perched on a limb of a breadfruit tree when a patrol of American soldiers elected to take a ten-minute break beneath it. Upon their departure, Ito dropped to the ground and grabbed the cigarette butts they'd left behind. Finding real cigarettes, even half-smoked ones, seemed a spectacu-lar stroke of good fortune, but not long afterward Ito and his two companions stopped smoking, despite the oc-casional availability not only of G.I. discards but of leaves from tobacco plants grown by the natives. "We came to realize that if we smoked, we wouldn't be able to smell other smokers' smoke as acutely," Ito says. "And it was important for us to be able to detect any other people in our vicinity before they detected us." Often the stragglers were forewarned of approaching Americans by a whiff of hair lotion. Once, at the U.S. Army dump, the stragglers unearthed a partly filled jar of pomade, and it took will power not to add that to their belongings, but they held back, reasoning that if they used it someone might get a whiff of them. They would go to the dump every week or so, just before dawn or just after dusk, and would fill some homemade knapsacks with empty cans and bottles, broken shovels and eating utensils, yards of mosquito net-ting, rags to patch their clothes with or to unravel for

thread, bedsprings to convert into needles, and empty
cartridge cases to turn into thimbles.

For several years, the three men periodically sharp-
ened old knives to a razor edge and shaved their beards
and cut their hair, but then they decided that the hairier
they got, the better protected their heads would be
against the ceaseless onslaughts of insects, and they gave
up their amateur barbering. While Guam's mosquitoes
are not malarial, they are multiple, and malign. If one of
the men slapped his forehead after dark, he was apt to
kill twenty mosquitoes. The netting they'd found at the
dump was torn, and thus far from mosquito-proof; when
they awoke at dawn, their palms would be red with blood.
They got inured to the insects' bites, but they continued
to slap away, out of fear that if they stopped they would
lose too much blood. The jungle also teemed with centipedes and with swarms of barely visible but savagely bit-
ing flying bugs, whose presence the Japanese blamed on
the Americans. There had been no such gadflies on Guam
when they first landed there, they reminded one another
bitterly; the pests had obviously been brought in by the
cursed Yankee invasion force.

On clear days, the stragglers would make a fire by
focussing the sun's rays through the bottom of a bottle.
For cloudy or rainy days, they soon learned—as other
stragglers on other Pacific islands were simultaneously
learning—another Promethean device. They would extract powder from unspent cartridges, mix it with dead
leaves or scraps of cloth, then rub a wire against a piece
of hardwood until the tip of the wire was hot enough to
spark the powder. The Japanese hadn't much other use

for the ammunition they picked up from time to time. They had rifles, but as a rule they used these only when they were desperately in want of meat, and even then they were careful never to hunt except during heavy rains, which dulled the sound of their firing. Back in 1945, Ito had taken from a dead soldier a rifle with eight rounds in its ammunition clip. In fifteen years, he fired just seven of the eight rounds. With his seven shots, he accounted for six cows and a wild pig. Another wild pig was secured for the stragglers' larder when they lurked in a tree beside one of its accustomed haunts and bashed it on the head with a rock as it sauntered by. Similarly, they once leaped from a tree onto the back of a deer whose meanderings they had reconnoitred, and wrestled it to earth. When they dressed the animal, they saved its stomach fluid, which, they had heard in their youth, made an excellent stomachic when dried. A pharmacological alternative was the dried liver of eels, which, along with crayfish, the Japanese trapped in the Tokui River. Unlike the majority of the stragglers elsewhere, these men never tried to grow anything; they lived off nature's or natives' bounty. Their staple foods, depending on the time of year, were bread-fruit, coconuts, papayas, and rose potatoes—these being potatolike root vegetables that grow on thorny vines. They ate rats, frogs, and snails as they chanced upon them. No matter how hungry Minagawa might be, he refused to eat lizards, which the three would now and then trap in a snare made out of wires salvaged from the dump; in Minagawa's home region, snakes were held in almost holy esteem, and he considered lizards familially close enough to snakes to merit respectful treatment.

OH, WHAT A MISERABLE LIFE THIS IS!

Whatever the stragglers had to eat, they were seldom entirely sated, and the division of their edible spoils
led to disputes. Unno thought that Ito ate too much.
Ito, the huskiest of the trio, admitted that he ate more
than the others, but pointed out that he knew his body
required the most fodder, so he always took pains to
gather extra food. He would add that it looked to him as
if Unno gathered precious little. "You want to eat more,
you work more," Ito recalls telling him. Minagawa kept
out of most of these spats, but he tended to sympathize
with Unno. To Minagawa's way of thinking, he and
Unno had done Ito a big favor by admitting him into
their household, and their graciousness merited his grati-
tude. Ito not only failed to be suitably appreciative,
Minagawa has subsequently declared, but was forever taking advantage of his superior strength to pick on Unno.

Unno was a lowly private, and Minagawa and Ito
were both a rank above him, but the senior member of
the group was Minagawa, who had nearly a year's more
service to his credit than Ito. If the three had rigidly observed Japanese military protocol, Minagawa would have
addressed Ito and Unno by their surnames alone, Unno
would have addressed his senior, Ito, as "Ito-*dono*," and
Ito would have addressed *his* senior, Minagawa, as "Mi-
nagawa-*dono*." (Japanese rarely use first names with non-
relatives, regardless of how closely they may be thrown
together.) The stragglers had agreed to waive these
niceties (although Minagawa thought he was giving the
others a break by condescending to such informality),
and it was as "Minagawa-san," "Ito-san," and "Unno-

san" that they equitably, though by no means always equably, conversed.

In the summer of 1950, the stragglers resolved, without acrimony, to try to escape from Guam. The Tokui flows into Ylig Bay, and from the cliffs above this harbor the trio had from time to time enviously watched Chamorro fishermen set forth after bonito, in sailboats a bit larger than rowboats. These craft looked eminently seaworthy, and the Japanese decided to steal one of them and aboard it sail the fifteen-hundred-mile stretch of ocean that separated them from home. They had no compass, but knew enough elementary astronomy to feel confident they could navigate by the stars. They reckoned that at night they would hoist a sail made out of tenting and by day, if any planes or ships came near, would pull the canvas down over them as a cloak. Spartanly, over the weeks that followed, they denied themselves food, until from even their meagre larder they had accumulated a tidy surplus, which they stored in old tin cans. They made fish hooks, with which they hoped to supplement their diet while afloat, and they counted on rain to provide them with water. They calculated that if all went according to plan they could reach Japan in about a month at the outside, and conceivably very much faster. Why, had not Ito been told by a civilian when he was on Saipan of a coconut that the ocean's mysterious currents had once wafted overnight from that island to Japan? Buoyed by this intelligence—about as wildly inaccurate as any intelligence could have been, although Ito passed it on in perfectly good faith—they were further enthused by the belief that the winds would speed them toward

Japan. Actually, if they had set sail in September or October, the prevailing winds would have pushed them northeast; if in November or later, southwest. Japan lies northwest of Guam, and at no time could their resolute cruise, had they embarked on it, have received a favorable breeze. But they did not know this. They thought their main difficulties would be getting a boat and, once in it, getting beyond the heavily patrolled shoreline. Late in the fall, they were ready. The day before they had scheduled their departure, a violent storm racked Guam. When they dragged their gear to the top of a cliff the following day, there wasn't a boat in sight. The entire fishing fleet had vanished—whether steered away or swept away they were never to know. Six months afterward, they returned to the place and once more scanned the harbor, but it was still bare of hulls. They abandoned that heady scheme forever.

One spring day in 1951, when the stragglers were hungrier, and hence edgier, than usual—it was the time of year when wild fruits were least abundant—they decided to move to a hill that they called Rose Mountain because its slopes were blanketed with flowers. There each man staked out a cave in which to keep personal possessions he did not use daily—extra cooking pots and tools, spare clothing, and so on. While Minagawa went off to collect some of his belongings, Ito and Unno got to squabbling along the old, familiar, contrapuntal lines: Ito was a glutton, Unno a drone; Ito, for a Johnny-come-lately, was too big for his breeches, Unno was far too outspoken for a man who didn't pull his weight. This time, the argument got out of hand.

Swearing angrily, Unno stalked off, and not long afterward Ito, hearing a noise behind him, turned to stare into the barrel of a rifle, levelled at him by Unno. Unno pulled the trigger, but there was only a click. He had taken Minagawa's weapon, and hadn't realized that the safety catch was on. Jumping at him, Ito knocked him down. Unno dropped the rifle, and they began to struggle hand to hand. Minagawa, returning, heard the commotion, ran up, and separated the two men. While the combatants glared at each other, he tried to make peace. "Nobody can live alone, so we all simply have to get along," he recalls admonishing them. Some face-saving was in order, he felt, so he continued, "Since I'm the responsible person here, I'll take the blame for what's just happened. I apologize to both of you, and I hope you can become friends."

It was a vain hope. For the next few months, the three men formed an uneasy triangle. Ito pitched a tent a hundred and fifty yards away from the other two—close enough to maintain contact, far enough away to shun intimacy. Night after night, he has said, he would be awakened by a noise. It was Unno, creeping toward his tent, a spear in his hand. Ito, who had no doubt he could whip Unno in a hand-to-hand fight, would cough menacingly, and Unno would slink away. Then, in a confidential chat with Minagawa, Ito said that maybe he ought to kill Unno before Unno caught him napping and killed *him*. (Ito has since said that he was only talking; he doesn't think he'd have gone through with it.) Minagawa replied that Unno had more than once nursed Ito when he was ill, and that a man just couldn't kill his benefactor. The

strain on all three became intolerable, and one day Unno
got his gear together and moved a mile or so away from
Ito and Minagawa—a vast distance, in jungle terms. Ito
didn't see him again for a year, but Minagawa, who still
had hopes of somehow effecting a reconciliation between
the others, would, without telling Ito, periodically drop
in on Unno and try to cheer him up.

One day, while Ito and Minagawa were sitting at
their camp site, Unno silently materialized. He was hol-
low-eyed, pale, and drawn. Without saying a word, he
began to erect a tent. "He looks bad," Minagawa said.
Ito nodded. When the tent was up, Unno fell onto his
back, exhausted, and started coughing. He said he must
have caught a cold, and would probably be all right in a
few days. He lay there, on a bed of leaves, for weeks.
Every so often, he would rise unsteadily and stagger off
to try to gather food, but he was too weak; Ito and Minagawa gave him some of their supplies. Unno's cough grew
worse. He complained of a buzzing in his ears, and said
his shoulders were sore and stiff. The others would mas-
sage him—Minagawa often and solicitously, Ito infre-
quently and stolidly. Soon Unno was too sick to eat. He
produced a stainless-steel razor he had fashioned from a
bread knife, handed it to Minagawa, and asked him to
cut his shoulders open and draw some blood, to relieve
the pain. Minagawa refused. The jungle, he said, was no
place for amateur blood-letting. But Unno begged and
begged, and finally Minagawa sliced one shoulder open
and cupped the incision with a bottle he'd heated to
create a vacuum. Black blood oozed forth. Unno's face
was drained of color, but he said he felt better, and he

pleaded for his other shoulder to be cut. This time, Ito wielded the razor. A few days later—it was, according to Ito's and Minagawa's computations, July 8, 1954—Unno stopped breathing. Minagawa snipped off some of Unno's hair and put it in a bottle, along with a slip of paper bearing his name and the words "Died on July 8, 1954, when the moon was half in the sky." The two survivors shaved the dead man's face, dressed him as neatly as they could, and dug a shallow grave. When they lifted his body, they were amazed at how little it weighed. With Unno they buried a few of his possessions—the razor, a sabre, a knife, a lens, a mirror, a pouch, and some needles and thread. They marked the grave with a log—though this constituted a breach of their policy never to leave any traces of their presence—and decorated the site with breadfruit and wild flowers. Then they placed the bottle containing Unno's hair and his epitaph in a cave, where it may still be.

Ito and Minagawa were alone. For nearly nine years they had been comrades, on and off, but almost always there had been somebody else around. Now the two of them were resigned to spending the rest of their time on earth together, however long that might be, and to living closer than brothers—closer, even, than most lovers— though they had neither affection nor respect for each other. Minagawa envied Ito his more imposing physique; Ito resented Minagawa's seniority in service. Minagawa's religious fervor, which at times became almost evangelical, irked Ito, a non-believer, who had had a bellyful of Minagawa's Buddha-is-my-copilot philosophy. Furthermore, Ito was still miffed because Minagawa, with Unno's sup-

port, had talked him out of responding to the leaflet from
the Repatriation Section the year before. Ito was sure he
would never have another chance to get in touch with the
outside world, and it was Minagawa, he reflected brood-
ingly, who had denied him his one shining opportunity.
But the chief thing that loomed between them was—and
still is—the shadow of Unno. Minagawa has never for-
given Ito for what he regards as the latter's inattentive,
even inhuman, attitude toward Unno. Ito was certainly
not fond of Unno; why should he have been, he asks,
when the man not only wouldn't do his share of the communal work but had homicidal designs upon him? In
1960, just before Ito and Minagawa were flown home
from Guam, Minagawa went back to Unno's grave and
dug up his bones, so he could deliver them to Unno's
family. Ito declined to go along.

Despite their differences, it was evident to both men
that neither could survive without the other, and in due
course they worked out a *mode de vie*, which they followed for their remaining six years in the jungle—a
period when, if either of them wanted the comfort or
counsel of another human being, he had nowhere to
turn but to the other. They would now and then discuss
the possibility of giving themselves up, in nighttime
conversations that more often than not ended with one
or the other exclaiming, "Oh, what a miserable life this
is!" On this point, they invariably saw eye to eye. Bad as
their life might be, however, both were positive that it
would be foolhardy to try to accost anyone else on the
island. (As late as 1957, a patrol opened fire on Ito while
he was gathering coconuts. Crouching and ducking, he

escaped through the underbrush, and discovered afterward that he had no more than a flesh wound from a bullet that creased his back.)

Ito and Minagawa could never be companionable or compatible, but they had to be coöperative. Their existence became one of detached togetherness. Every six months or so, they would move, mainly to seek untapped sources of food. Wherever they chose to stop, they occupied separate tents. Each man had his own tools and implements, his own clothes and repair kits. Each gathered his own staple food, and cooked his own meals—usually at dawn—over his own fire. Whenever either man found something special, though—a pig, a chicken, a crab, or some other treat—it was divided in two. Together they would raid the dump. Together they would go to the seashore every couple of months to fetch water they could convert, by boiling or evaporation, into salt. Together they rigged a fresh-water tank out of a discarded American tire tube. And when one was sick, the other ministered to him.

At times when they had enough food and there were no pressing chores to do, Ito and Minagawa would sit near their shelters and talk about their families. On rare occasions, when they were feeling exceptionally relaxed and cordial, they would reminisce jokingly about girls they had slept with, in a time so long past that it hardly seemed real, but even during the most hilarious confessions they never dared laugh aloud; there was no way of telling who might hear them and pounce in the dark. Actually, sex did not much occupy their thoughts. "We were always scared of being killed," Minagawa says, "and in those circumstances we hadn't much time to worry about women." Once, in the pages of an old magazine, they came across a naked woman's photograph. Using the picture as his model, Ito whittled an eight-inch-high nude, but shortly afterward he became conscious that he had begun talking to this wooden image, so he threw it into a fire. Self-restraint, he knew, was the overriding order of the day.

Minagawa knew this well, too. "I don't think those sixteen years on Guam were a waste of time, because they made me able to stand anything," he said afterward. "Whenever I get angry now, I can control myself. In that respect, at least, my life may be happier today than it would have been if I'd come home at the end of the war. You know, it's easy to raise your standard of living, but terribly hard to lower it. The most important thing that happened to me in these sixteen years was learning to endure the very lowest standard of living imaginable and the very harshest of disciplines—self-discipline." If the two Guamanian crab hunters had not chanced to leave Talofofo early that morning in 1960, Minagawa and Ito might still be testing their remarkable endurance.

American soldiers long encamped on foreign soil traditionally proclaim that when they return home they will kiss the ground, or eat some of their mother's homemade blueberry pie, or engage in some similar ethnic ceremonial. When Minagawa returned home, he wanted mainly to see his sister; he said in the Naval Hospital at Guam that if he could just have a look at her he would be content to die. Ito (who, incidentally, doubts whether any American would have had the physical or mental fortitude to go through what he went through, and who remarks rather scornfully that in 1941, when the Japanese took Guam, many Americans surrendered with excessive alacrity) had been nursing one American-style hope all along. He had a hankering for a bowl of *misoshiru*—a spicy Japanese soup made from bean paste, fish, vegetables, and various fiery condiments. He gobbled some *misoshiru* on his first night in Japan.

At a homecoming press conference that the stragglers held at Tachikawa, it was Ito who did most of the talking, though he spoke so softly and stuttered so badly that he couldn't be heard very well. Minagawa, whose luggage consisted mainly of Unno's bones, encased in a box the Navy had given him and wrapped in clean white cloth, was dazed. "I just can't understand anything," one reporter quoted him as saying. In a subsequent, ghost-written book of memoirs, he characterized his feelings in somewhat more soaring prose: "I felt like a bird without a tree to perch on." Both men, naturally, were confounded by their first views of their homeland. Neither had ever been to Tokyo before, and they expected to find the capital of a nation whose soldiers had unforgivably lost the war a devastated shambles. Instead, they gaped at the world's biggest metropolis—a stunning, bulging, deafening beehive of modernity. A few days after their return, thousands of university students and other young people demonstrated riotously against the government of Nobusuke Kishi, then the Prime Minister. Ito and Minagawa took in some of these turbulent performances and were flabbergasted. "I can't understand what this big fuss is all about," Ito said. Minagawa, gazing at young Japanese women with hennaed hair and painted fingernails who strolled hand in hand with men, simply refused to believe that these bizarre-looking and acting females were not foreigners. Later, as the men browsed through Japanese newspapers, both of them were puzzled by a host of English words transliterated into Japanese—"sex," "teen-ager," "strikeout," "love scene," "missile," and so on. They had come back to a world that made no sense.

On Guam, Minagawa and Ito had suggested to Edward Tsutsui that, in the improbable event that they were not executed or imprisoned, maybe he could get them jobs on that island; they were appalled by the prospect of returning to their homeland in defeat. Now they were further bewildered when the Japanese press showered on them the sort of acclaim that is usually reserved for victors. *Asahi*, not content with having obtained a firsthand journalistic account of their saga on Guam, grabbed up their own first-person accounts, and both men found themselves spending more time with scribbling journalists than with their families. Ito's autobiography was on sale in book form less than a month after he had sucked in his first serving of *misoshiru*. Meanwhile, a widely circulated weekly magazine came up with an apocryphal story headed "Straggler Reports to the Emperor," in which Ito (whose first name the magazine muffed) introduced himself thus:

Your Majesty, Imperial Army Sergeant Tadashi Ito reports to you. I have just returned from duty.

The imaginary interview continued with Ito's delivery of a brisk chastisement to the Emperor—an impertinence for which at the time he joined the Army he could have been beheaded.

> Why, why did Japan lose the war? I believed in your divinity, but I no longer believe in you. It was your sole responsibility that you waged a war you never had a chance to win.
>
> I feel very sad. I held out in the jungle firmly believing that someday the Japanese Army would come to relieve me. Why, why did Japan lose the war? . . .
>
> I felt like an insane man. I felt really ashamed to come home disgracefully alive while all my comrades-in-arms died honorably in combat. I don't want the people to welcome me as if I were a hero.
>
> It was only my duty to hold out in the jungle until reinforcements arrived. This was by no means a heroic deed. In sixteen years I have forgotten almost everything, but I can still recite, word for word, your Imperial rescript to your soldiers: "Do not disgrace yourself by being captured alive, but die."
>
> I was loyal to your rescript. And by observing it I have wasted my youth in the dark jungle.

The Imperial Household Agency, which handles relations between the Emperor and his subjects, was asked to comment on this soldierly gripe, but it kept silent. Ito didn't comment, either, at the time, but he has subsequently denied that he ever composed a word of the rebuke attributed to him.

The American doctors on Guam had pronounced Ito and Minagawa to be in reasonably good health, but

OH, WHAT A MISERABLE LIFE THIS IS!

now the pair accepted the invitation of the indefatigable
Asahi to be its guests for an all-expenses-paid, three-week
sojourn at the Keio University Hospital, in Tokyo. The
stragglers had adjoining private rooms, but though they
were ambulatory patients, they hardly ever visited each
other. (A woman who had read of their vicissitudes sent
some pocket money in an envelope addressed to Minagawa. An *Asahi* man suggested that he give Ito half.
Minagawa was willing, but Ito wouldn't take it.) The
two men had few callers from outside. *Asahi*, which had
obtained from the hospital the exclusive right to publish
the findings of all the internists, dermatologists, oph-
thalmologists, dentists, orthopedists, laryngologists, psychologists, and psychiatrists who examined the pair,
wanted no one hanging around who might interfere with
its clinical scoop. Ito and Minagawa were compliant
enough about most of the poking and prodding to which
they were subjected, but Ito—conceivably meditating on
the death of Unno—complained that the doctors were
taking too many blood specimens.

Both men were self-conscious about being tended
by women on the hospital staff. When a woman psychologist visited each, in turn, to give them some intelligence and aptitude tests, each was embarrassed and
disturbed at being alone in a room with her. (The psychiatrists, being psychiatrists, naturally searched with all
the recondite resources at their disposal for evidence of
latent or outright homosexuality. They found not a trace
of it.) At one point, the woman psychologist dropped
in on Ito to evaluate his ability to cope with elementary
arithmetical problems. Ito lapsed into surly silence after

the first few questions. He later said all the numbers made him dizzy. "I don't know why," he told *Asahi*, "but I just couldn't answer an easy question like 'What is left if fifteen is taken three times from one hundred?' I didn't have to do that sort of thing in the jungle."

A psychiatrist subsequently explained Ito's blankness as "a deterioration of mental ability because of situational factors." The over-all psychiatric analysis of both men was that they were absolutely normal, though a mite wary and insecure and not particularly adept at coming to grips with abstractions. But then, the psychiatrists noted, how many Japanese farm lads who simply stayed home were particularly adept at coming to grips with abstractions? While the stragglers were being interviewed by the doctors, the faintest noise in the corridor outside their rooms would distract them, and they were also uncommonly sensitive to any intrusive odor—"a manifestation," one of the psychiatrists said, "of their defensive attitude toward outside aggressions." Both men, the doctors noted, would awaken every morning at four o'clock, out of seemingly unbreakable habit. (They now sleep longer.) One difference between them during their hospital sojourn was that Minagawa would eat anything set before him, while Ito spurned all raw foods.

Psychiatry is not an especially advanced branch of medical science in Japan today, and the observations made of Ito and Minagawa were fairly superficial. Still, these two men, in contradistinction to other stragglers from other areas, were at least examined. The doctors were hampered somewhat in their efforts by a lack of any reliable criteria against which to measure their findings on the pair; but the doctors were nonetheless convinced that neither man exhibited any pathological symptoms. This negative, relatively tame conclusion came as a disappointment to some other Japanese psychiatrists, who yawned with boredom when one of the Keio doctors, at a professional symposium, delivered a paper on the two Guam stragglers; his colleagues seemed to feel that any pair of individuals who had undergone so unusual an experience should have developed some diverting psychoses.

Physically, the two checked out in tiptop shape, all things considered. Minagawa was slightly astigmatic, and glasses were prescribed for him. His spine was a bit curved, from his life as a bearded snail, and the onerous jungle years had also caused the edges of both men's bone joints to become sharp. Both had a mild calcium deficiency, but the Keio dentists pronounced them astounding oral specimens, saying that their teeth were no worse, and perhaps a little better, than those of most Japanese males of their age. Ito and Minagawa, the dentists were pleased to learn, had always tried, with whatever equipment was at hand, to brush their teeth at least once daily.

The two men were released from the hospital in mid-July of 1960, and then were faced with the problem of supporting themselves. They had received some money from *Asahi* and other publishers, and they had also received forty thousand yen each in back Army pay, computed on ˙ wartime scale; but the yen, which had been worth eighty-four cents when they went off to battle, was now worth less than three, so for sixteen years of faithful service to the Emperor they received just over a hundred dollars apiece. It was not much of a grubstake, and for men around forty, without vocational experience, jobs were not easy to come by. But Hiroshi Okawa, the president of the Toei Motion Picture Company, who, like Minagawa, was a native of Niigata Prefecture, offered the latter a watchman's job at the Toei lot, on the northern edge of Tokyo. A few days later, having decided to make a movie about the stragglers, and figuring that it would be convenient to have both of them available for technical advice, Toei offered Ito a similar job. (Minagawa again held seniority, and was aware of it.) Thus, the unfriendly intimates once again found themselves together. At the studio, where they are still employed, they seldom meet. They are on different shifts, so as a rule they see each other on the lot only at eight o'clock in the morning, the time of the changing of the Toei guard.

The movie about them, *Saigo No Nihon-hei* ("The Last of the Imperial Army"), was released in October, 1960. The characters based on Ito and Minagawa bore their real-life names, but Unno was called Takano, because the producers felt that the use of his name might cause his family unnecessary distress. In some respects, the script stuck exceedingly close to the facts; for instance, the actor who portrayed Ito affected a stutter, though it was a more aggravated stutter than Ito's. But there were also quite a few instances of dramatic license. Ito was shown sobbing convulsively on Unno's—or Takano's—grave, and Ito and Minagawa were shown splashing noisily as they bathed in the sea. During their sixteen years on Guam, they would have regarded any such clamorous commotion as suicidal. *Saigo No Nihon-hei* did not make itself much of a splash at the box office. A large proportion of the movie-goers in Japan, as elsewhere nowadays, are teen-agers, and this influential segment of the audience was not awfully eager to take in an eighty-seven-minute picture—even one shot in ToeiScope—about a minor episode in an ancient war on an all but unheard-of island called Guam.

For a while, both Ito and Minagawa lived in a dormitory that Toei maintains near its lot for its un-married male employees. Ito moved out at the end of 1960, and on January 7, 1961, two months before his fortieth birthday, he got married. His bride, Taeko Endo, who was twenty-nine at the time, is the third daughter of a fruit-store proprietor; she was working as a secretary when they got married. The Itos live in an eight-by-ten-foot one-room apartment in Itabashi, a district in northern Tokyo. Theirs is a plain, unexciting, typical lower-mid-dle-class Japanese existence. When a recent visitor to Ito's home asked him if he still pursued his hobby of carving, he replied—it seemed almost wistfully—"Carving takes time, and I have no time these days. I'm always spending my time with somebody else." Ito has an infant girl now; so has Minagawa. Minagawa's sister had announced as soon as news of his rescue reached her that she was going to find him a nice bride, but shortly after Ito's wedding he found one on his own—Hiyomi Jinnai, who, as it happened, was also a twenty-nine-year-old third daughter. She became Minagawa's wife on April 2, 1961, when he was forty, and they live in a rented room in the Nerima section of Tokyo, not far from the Toei studios. Neither straggler attended his comrade's wedding.

3

EVEN
IF IT TAKES
A HUNDRED YEARS

On August 15, 1945, when Emperor Hirohito of Japan made his radio début to tell his subjects they had lost the Second World War, some six and a half-million Japanese soldiers, sailors, and civilian employees of the armed forces were outside their country's home islands, scattered from remote Pacific atolls to Southeast Asia, China, and Siberia. Five years later, three hundred and sixty-seven thousand of these people had still not been repatriated—the vast majority of them being in Soviet and Chinese prison camps. Between 1950 and 1960, most of the prisoners of war were returned home. (The Japanese government claims that even now twenty thousand ex-servicemen are involuntarily detained on the mainland by the Communists. The Communists, for their part, insist that they currently hold only a handful of hard-core war criminals.) In addition to prisoners, there have been some more unusual categories of long-term Japanese absentees. Some of them are men who elected to stay where they were when the war ended, and decided that they preferred life overseas—say, farming in Sumatra—to the life they had known in Japan. Others were men who just didn't get around to coming home for a while—men like Tsunekichi Matsuda, who went to Vietnam in 1941 as a medical orderly; who hung around after V-J Day long enough to be accepted as a full-fledged doctor, marry a Vietnamese girl, and father six children; and who then, in 1960, returned to Tokyo, where the best job he could find was a menial one in a department store, where his wife took ill with a nervous ailment, and the change of climate caused one of their children to die of pneumonia. Even after Matsuda's belated and discouraging reappearance, there showed up in Tokyo one Genzo Seki, whose family believed he had died when a troop transport on which he was proceeding from Saipan to Guam, in 1944, had been sunk. Seki, however, had swum to Saipan, lived in a cave there for two years, and, on being captured by an American Army patrol in 1946, had identified himself as a Chinese. He thereupon went to work in a United States military hospital, married a Saipan woman, and, by the time he got around to notifying his kinsfolk in Japan he was still alive, had two children, aged thirteen and eleven.

Of all the dawdling expatriates, those who have most interested the Japanese public have been the former service people who, like Ito and Minagawa, didn't get back home until long, long after the war was over for very different reasons—because they didn't know that the war had ended, didn't believe that it had ended, or, having heard that it had, were either ashamed to return home in defeat or fearful of the treatment they would receive at the hands of the victors—an understandable apprehension in view of the way many Japanese soldiers had treated *their* prisoners. In the first few years after the war, hundreds of such *zanryūsha* were flushed out of their lairs. What is more remarkable is that in the years *since* 1950 about forty more diehard stragglers have turned up. Few Japanese would bet that the two found alive on Guam in May of 1960 are the last of an odd lot. The Pacific islands embrace hundreds of thousands of square miles of sparsely populated and scarcely penetrable land, and if, in this temperate, though inhospitable, environment, a man is able to find enough food and water, and does not succumb to injury or illness, he can theoretically live, or at any rate exist, until he dies of old age. Thus, in the event that a Third World War should start in the next couple of decades, and spread over the Pacific, it is possible—if not very probable—that it might involve some dogged Japanese who thought they were still fighting the Second.

Despite their having held onto life so tenaciously under such dispiriting circumstances, not all the stragglers have been pleased at being returned to the company of civilized men. Two *zanryūsha* who withstood the jungle of the Philippines for, respectively, eleven and twelve years committed suicide while in comparatively comfortable Manila prison cells, awaiting investigation of their status. Another straggler whose survival was more unusual killed himself in a more unusual way. He was Kofuku Yamakage, one of a pair of Japanese marines who somehow survived the battle of Iwo Jima, in which twenty-three thousand of their compatriots were annihilated, and who remained in a cave there for five years until they gave themselves up. In 1951, jobless in Tokyo, Yamakage ran into Stuart Griffin, subsequently a columnist there for the English-language daily *Mainichi*, and at that time an American military historian. Griffin learned that the former marine had left a diary on Iwo Jima, and persuaded its author to go back there with him to retrieve it. Yamakage poked at the slopes of Mount Suribachi for a while, and then, failing to unearth his journal, suddenly screamed "Banzai!" and leapt off that celebrated hill to his death. It had depressed him, Griffin later reported, to return to the scene of his anguish and to reflect that, of all the Japanese who'd gone to Iwo Jima, he was so uncommonly viable.

While none of the stragglers who have made it back to Japan have come close to matching Robinson Crusoe's record of twenty-eight years of enisled living, it must be remembered that Daniel Defoe's hero had a shipload of tools and other gear, to say nothing a man Friday, and, most important, he was not at war with anybody, or under the impression that he was. "Robinson Crusoe," in translation, is staple fare in many Japanese schools, and a few of the stragglers either had read it before they took to the bushes or have browsed through it since their return. Their consensus is that Crusoe had things much easier than they did. Ito has never read the book but has heard about it, and he says, "If there hadn't been soldiers or natives chasing me all the time, my sixteen years would have passed easily enough, but I always had to face the possibility of being shot, so I think my life was harder than Crusoe's."

Nearly all the stragglers, like Crusoe, had long since been given up for dead by their kin, and nearly all had been given war heroes' funerals *in absentia*. A school-master named Shigeichi Yamamoto, one of four men who were plucked off a mountainside on the Philippine island of Mindoro in October, 1956, has put together a personal scrapbook dealing with his adventure and its aftermath, and the very first picture in the collection is a snapshot of him kneeling in prayer beside his own grave. After making and recording this obeisance, however, Yamamoto uprooted his headstone and sold it. Recarved, it now marks a neighboring grave. Other stragglers have reacted to their own memorials in varying ways. The seventh, thirteenth, and twenty-first anniversaries of a death are important in Japan, and are observed with solemn ceremonies. One of Yamamoto's comrades on Mindoro, Seiji Izumida, got home just in time to fore-stall his thirteenth-anniversary rites. After calling them off, he dug up his gravestone, and found buried beneath it a box full of rotted material. Without inquiring of his family what had been put in the box, he threw it away, but he thriftily saved the stone, which he plans to use again when it is indisputably needed. Keishichi Kishi, another straggler who returned to Japan in 1956, from the island of Morotai, in the Moluccas, took even more forthright measures to obliterate the evidence of his demise. He collected all the documents pertaining to it and set fire to them, then slapped red paint across the inscription on his gravestone. The day after Ito's return from Guam, he exchanged his new Western suit for a kimono and, carrying a parasol, paid a formal call on his grave. He hasn't disturbed it in any way; he plans to leave it as it is, and, when he dies, to have a second stone put up. "That first grave is for the death of my soldier's life," he says.

In contrast to Minagawa, who resisted capture by the Guamanian crab-hunters because he thought they were out to kill him, other stragglers had to be forcibly dealt with for the reason that they construed it as their soldierly duty to wage war forever. The fact that Japanese soldiers were so thoroughly indoctrinated has given rise to postwar soul-searching. "We must study with deep consciousness the inhuman teachings of the old Japanese militarists," *Mainichi* said editorially in 1960. Such a study is complicated by the fact that not all the precepts of the old militarists were conducive to, or even consistent with, a straggling way of life. Many Japanese soldiers were told on the eve of battle that their only honorable alternatives were those set forth in the Bushido code—victory or death. In defeat, a man who was not physically incapacitated was supposed to kill himself. Regardless of the means he chose—a suicidal banzai attack, hara-kiri, clutching a live hand grenade to his chest—the end was prescribed, and the reward was generous and glorious: a soldier who died at his post would at once become deified, and thereby attain an affinity with his Emperor that he could never aspire to while alive. By the old, traditional Bushido standards, the most resourceful and resilient straggler, no matter how ghastly the hardships he had undergone, would have been esteemed considerably beneath a soldier who had put the barrel of a pistol in his mouth and pulled the trigger. This explains why some stragglers, unaware of how much Japan had changed in their absence, were reluctant to come

home; though lucky to be alive, they were chagrined at
their own egregious vitality.

But Japan, of course, *had* changed, and not merely
in respect to such things as Western clothes, modern
buildings, and jazz music. Many of the stragglers were
astonished to be received with adulation and hailed in the
press with high-flown phrases like "living spirits of
heroes." There have been innumerable newspaper and
magazine articles about the hardy species, not to mention a spate of autobiographies, most of them hastily
written "as-told-to" potboilers. (The few stragglers who
have ploddingly penned their memoirs themselves have
had little success peddling them; in Japan, as in the
Western world it emulates, living spirits of heroes stand
a better chance of getting their stories published if they
work through ghosts.) Ito and Minagawa each had had a
book published, and the movie about their tribulations
had been on view, before they'd been home five months.
At the studio where they are employed as watchmen,
they are considered exceptionally well qualified for this
work; a man who has spent sixteen years constantly
listening for the click of a rifle bolt or the snap of a twig
has achieved an alertness nearly as keen and sweeping as
that of radar.

Ito and Minagawa now exhibit few outward signs
of jumpiness. Indeed, they seem surprisingly calm—almost phlegmatic. They are sometimes asked by sightseers visiting the Toei lot, or by other random acquaintances, what effects their long estrangement from civilization has had on them. They usually reply—and so do most
of the other stragglers to whom the question is put—that

just about the only significant change they can detect in themselves is a marked enhancement of self-control. "I have learned to be patient," Ito says. "I have learned to be coöperative. I can restrain myself better than I'd have been able to otherwise. Now I don't—in fact, I simply can't—say exactly what I feel, and I can't do exactly what I want to do. These days, in Japan, everybody seems to say what he wants to say and do what he wants to do. I can't. Of course, it could be that I am old-fashioned."

Most of the stragglers showed exceptional patience almost from the start of their detached existence. They were prepared to stay wherever they were—a cave on Guam, a cliff on Saipan, a grass hut in New Guinea, or a crude lean-to in the Philippines—for as long as they could breathe. Minagawa recalls that on Guam, before he joined up with Ito, a Japanese officer pointed out to him and some other soldiers that since it had taken the United States, for all its vaunted might, two and a half years to recapture Guam, it might very well take the Japanese even longer to rerecapture it. "In three years or so, the Japanese Army will come back for you," Minagawa quotes the officer as saying in 1944, "and in the meantime you wait and help each other out, no matter what. Remember, you are Japanese soldiers." The officer and all the other men involved in this colloquy are now presumed dead; Minagawa alone remembers.

Some of the stragglers remained incredibly soldierly right up to the moment when they were discovered and disarmed. Kishi, the man who returned from Morotai in

1956, had been a corporal, and the highest-ranking member of a group of nine men on that Moluccan island. When, in November of 1955, an Indonesian policeman caught up with him on a beach there, and asked if he had any weapons, Kishi acknowledged that he had a rifle and some ammunition stashed in the underbrush. On being told to go get them and yield them up, Kishi retorted that he'd die first. What was more, it soon developed that each of the eight men with him had a rifle, and each had been ordered by Kishi never to have less than a hundred rounds of ammunition at the ready, even if this meant curtailing the hunt for food. "I made my men keep their rifles clean at all times, because I wanted to be prepared for combat at any time," the corporal has since said. "Our last formal order had been to stand by, and I told my men, 'Sooner or later the Japanese Army will come back, even if it takes a hundred years.'" Ultimately, Kishi agreed to accompany the Indonesian policeman back toward civilization, but only on condition that the stragglers be permitted to retain their arsenal until they met up with some Japanese authorities who could officially inform them that the war was over and instruct them to lay down their arms. Nearly two months elapsed before this came to pass—at the Japanese consulate in Djakarta—and even then, a decade after Japan's surrender, Kishi slowed down the proceedings by insisting that he be allowed to count his men's bullets. When the inventory had been taken, he announced with pride that the total was just a few short of nine hundred, and then demanded that the Japanese consul give him a written receipt for the ammunition. "I wanted to have proof that we had never lost our fighting spirit," he says.

On September 15, 1944, General Douglas Mac-Arthur's forces landed on Morotai, which lies two hundred and fifty miles south of Mindanao, in the Philippines, and which MacArthur's staff visualized as a handy base for fighter planes engaged in the reconquest of those islands. In late November, to prevent Morotai's being used for this purpose, the Japanese sent twenty-five hundred men from nearby Halmahera to retake the island. Most of these soldiers either were killed in action or died of starvation or disease. The remnants took to the bush. The indomitable Kishi was twenty-four at the time. A native of Yamagata Prefecture, a predominantly agricultural region a couple of hundred miles north of Tokyo, he had gone to Manchuria in 1939 as a junior economist, had enlisted in the Army there, and had been trained as a cipher clerk—an occupational specialty that was of singularly little use to him when he and his men were cut off from all channels of communication. The only human beings the group had any contact with after its first few months on Morotai were a family of natives Kishi ran into on the eve of his capture. In November, 1955, his men were so hungry for at least a scrap of information about the world beyond their jungle that he decided they would go to the coast—a three-day trip by raft down an inland river—to see what they could see. En route, he bumped into a native woman with a child, and then her husband turned up. In sign language, Kishi asked if the natives had seen any Americans, and on being told that they hadn't, he indicated that his party

was going to push on to the seashore in search of further
intelligence. The natives, who knew the terrain better
than the Japanese did, took a short cut to the coast and,
once there, sounded the alarm. The Indonesian police
were waiting for Kishi when, leaving his men as well as
his rifle concealed in the woods, he came into the open.

Shortly after their life of waiting began, Kishi's
group had met up with some other Japanese, who had
passed along a rumor that a ship would be coming to the
mouth of a nearby river to evacuate all the Japanese on
Morotai. Going to the designated spot, Kishi's men, who
then numbered eleven, found no boat but merely a
swarm of other Japanese drawn to the place by the same
fantasy. Kishi judged that there was too little food in the
area to sustain that large a crowd, so he and his men
moved away. For the next year or so, they prowled around
aimlessly, scrounging whatever edibles—coconuts, papayas,
grasshoppers, and so forth—they could lay their hands on,
and during this period two of the eleven men fell ill
and died. The rest, all of whom were ultimately rescued
with Kishi, were Masao Akagi, of Okayama; Takeo Ha-
rada, of Nara; and six Formosans—Hajime Motoyama,
Tomeo Maeda, Jirou Yoshia, Tomeo Wakayama, Tarou
Nishimura, and Yasuichi Kuniyama. In time, the nine
men came upon a cultivated field, which had been planted
with sweet-potato vines and tapioca and papaya sprouts,
and then, apparently, abandoned. They decided to settle
in the forest nearby, and they built a shack. Thereafter,
most days, from dawn to dusk, were spent searching for
frogs, snakes, wild boars, and other items to supplement
their monotonous diet. Whatever any of them brought

back would be handed over to Kishi, who would scrupulously divide the food into nine parts, and would make
a point, if one portion seemed a trifle undersized, of taking that one for himself. Each morning and each evening,
the stragglers lit cooking fires, using flints, or else rubbing
sticks together. For pots, they had American helmets
they'd picked up. (As cooking utensils, these were far
superior to Japanese helmets, which had four ventilation
holes in them.) By day, the men went nearly naked,
saving their ragged uniforms to wear during the relative
cool of the night; eventually, they supplanted the uniforms with clothes and sandals that they wove from
hemp. After dark, Kishi would try to perk up his crew
by narrating fanciful stories of how Japan had won the
war. If his auditors suggested that such an outcome
seemed little short of miraculous, he would remind them
that an apparently successful Mongol invasion of Japan
in the thirteenth century had been repelled, according
to the tale their ancestors had handed down, by gods
called *kami*, who had stirred up a violent wind called a
kaze. Who among them, he would sternly ask, was
prescient enough to say for sure that within the next
hundred years or thereabouts Japan would not once again
be providentially rid of its oppressors?

Kishi arrived back in Japan on March 19, 1956. He
has since married and is now the father of a young son.
He lives in Tokyo, where he works in a foundry. Though
there is nothing specifically wrong with his health, he
feels that his eleven years in the jungle sapped his
energy, and at last report he was looking for a desk job.
He was also looking for somebody to publish a three-

hundred-page "Robinson Crusoe"-like saga he had written, but was not overly dejected at having found no takers. "I have a strong conviction that after what I went through nothing can ever get me down again," he said recently.

At one time on Morotai, Kishi and his men were on such intolerably short rations that they toyed with the idea of raiding a native village that they thought might be richly stocked. They dismissed the notion, though, upon reflecting that it was one thing to continue an old war with Americans who might be far away, but quite another to start a new war with natives over the next hill. Such caution was characteristic of most of the stragglers, and it helped account for the success of their long disappearing acts. Many Japanese are fond of seclusion while at home and at peace, and in the Pacific wilds the strays often went to great lengths to avoid any contact with strangers. Nevertheless, on most of the islands where they are known or are assumed to have hidden, it has become a postwar gambit for parents to curb unruly children by warning them that if they don't behave, a Japanese straggler will get them. On the island of Truk, where no flesh-and-blood straggler has yet been apprehended, a phantom straggler has entered the folklore—a solitary, bearded cave dweller who reputedly, after scaring the daylights out of miscreant youngsters, becomes invisible if anybody takes a step toward him. He is a particularly unlikely spectre, if only because few of the men who have straggled for any appreciable length of time have done so in solitude; indeed, the handful who have voluntarily given themselves up have, in almost every instance, done so because they were companionless. Typical of these was Kaichiro Eguchi, who, on June 13, 1953, astonished the villagers of Ginagaya, a settlement a hundred miles southeast of Manila, by suddenly appearing in their midst. A private first class, Eguchi had stumbled into the hills with four other men in 1944, when their unit fell apart. Subsequently, two of the four had died of malaria, and the other two had disappeared. Eguchi was left pretty well fixed. He had some quinine, a rifle, and a hundred rounds of ammunition. He had ready access to fruits and vegetables, lobsters and fish, and wild pigs and rabbits, not to mention an occasional chicken from a Luzon farm. He had made himself some passable clothes from hemp fibre, and had fitted them out with coconut-shell buttons. But he couldn't go it alone. More than once, as the years dragged by, he had crept close to a native compound, planning to give himself up. But each time he had stolen silently away, purely for lack of sufficient nerve to accost another human being. When he could finally stand it no more, he walked into Ginagaya. Upon being asked what had brought him there, he said, "I wanted a man to talk to."

Throughout the Pacific islands, there have been many more alleged stragglers than real ones. Every so often, a pilot flying over a stretch of uncharted jungle will see some newish-looking huts, and a new rumor will soon be airborne. At least three widely separated islands have been claimed to harbor a legendary unwashed Japanese soldier, who, just after the war, supposedly spent months in an American Army encampment, sleeping by

day under the floor of a tent and emerging at night to
attend the outdoor movies; the story goes that he was
exposed when a G.I. noticed that the fellow sitting beside
him in the dark smelled excessively bad. In the last
couple of years, the Solomon Islands have been the
source of several rumors. On Guadalcanal, there is supposed to dwell a brutal, barefoot, fast-striding fellow
who likes to attack natives; people who believe he is real
also believe him to be a Formosan, since the Formosans
are noted for their fleetness of foot while unshod. However, nobody on Guadalcanal has yet found a persuasive
footprint. In 1959, on nearby Vella Lavella, possible
factual evidence of straggler activity was discovered. A
woman there said she had seen seven or eight wild-look-
ing Japanese on the loose, and when the local police went
out to investigate, they did turn up an empty bottle
that had once contained Asahi beer, a popular Japanese
brand. But there was no way of telling when and by
whom the contents had been consumed. Bougainville
is thought to shelter a single Japanese Army captain;
Borneo, three Japanese soldiers of unknown rank. The
Philippine Islands are big, and have spawned big rumors.
Cebu has been credited with thirty stragglers, Leyte with
thirty-five. A Japanese officer and two hundred enlisted
men are reported to have settled in the wilds of Mindanao, married native women, and raised families, but
when, in the summer of 1960, the Japanese Embassy in
Manila sent an expedition out to hunt for them, the
searchers came back empty-handed. Almost everywhere
that the Japanese were—and in the course of trying to
establish their Greater East Asia Co-Prosperity Sphere

they covered a lot of ground—Japanese are rumored still to be.

Rumors aside, enough genuine stragglers have turned up to make anyone hesitate to scoff at reports of still more. In 1955, the remote island of Peleliu yielded up a chap who differed from most of his straggling brethren in that, although he had been living alone for the better part of ten years, he was nonetheless far from willing to rejoin the society of men. Some natives on Peleliu had been aware of periodic filching of their tapioca, and on the evening of April 28, 1955, three local boys in one of the fields saw some tapioca leaves shaking violently, as if they were being uprooted. The boys gave chase, and a man scurried off. They presently caught up with, and wrestled into submission, one Keiki Tokugawa, a farmer from Korea who had been conscripted by the Japanese Army back in 1942 to work in a Peleliu phosphate mine. Tokugawa had fled to the hills in September, 1944, when United States forces landed on the island, and had stayed in hiding, unmoved by placards nailed to trees and by jeeps tooling up and down the roads broadcasting appeals to him and anyone else who might be within earshot to come out, come out, wherever they were.

Three years before Tokugawa was bagged, the island of Saipan had produced a brace of almost equally elusive birds. Early one morning, a farmer spotted a naked man scrambling up the side of a hundred-foot cliff, and notified the local authorities of this spectacularly unconventional performance. The police, sneaking around to the back of the cliff and going up the easy way, bagged two soldiers named Toshiyoshi Ide and Toshiji Kamigawara, who had been living on the cliff top like eagles in an aerie. Every four or five days, they would scramble down to forage for food—fresh-water eels, fat land snails, mangoes, papayas, rats. They cooked on a fire they lit from the spark gap of an old electric generator, seasoning their food with salt they obtained by letting sea water evaporate, and with sugar they obtained by smashing sugar cane with a rusty pair of pliers. For recreation, they snared wild canaries and bred them. Eight years and nobody could guess how many canaries after they first occupied their roost, Ide and Kamigawara were brought south to Guam and thence returned to Japan.

Just north of Saipan lies the island of Anatahan, which produced a couple of dozen stragglers, among them the only woman more or less eligible for the designation. Anatahan was never the scene of wartime fighting, but in June, 1944, a convoy of Japanese ships was bombed by American planes off its shores. Several of the ships were sunk, and thirty-one survivors—about half of them soldiers, half sailors—swam to Anatahan. The Japanese government had a civilian overseer there, a man named Kikuichiro Higa, who supervised the activities of some seventy native farmers. He, in turn, had an Okinawan deputy with the same surname, Shoichi Higa, whose wife, Kazuko, was also there. Shortly after the castaways reached Anatahan, Shoichi went off on an inspection trip to a neighboring island, and that was the last anybody on Anatahan heard of him. Kikuichiro Higa then moved in with his namesake's wife, and they lived together until 1947, when Kikuichiro died of an unspecified disease. Meanwhile, the native farmers had been taken off Anatahan during one of several periodic sorties that United States forces made to the spot. Whenever the Americans landed, the Japanese would flee inland and hide. The rest of the time, they busied themselves growing bananas and a kind of coarse local potato called the pig potato, trapping lizards, and fishing for sharks. After each American visit, the Japanese would collect the cigarette butts left behind and have a party, livening things up with liquor they had made from coconut juice.

After Mrs. Higa became mateless for the second time, the captain of one of the foundered ships took charge of the island colony. Apparently hoping that a married woman would cause less trouble than a widow among so many men, he ordered her to take as husband a young straggler named Yanagihashi. Mrs. Higa assented. About two months later, the captain disappeared, and so did Yanagihashi. After that, there is some confusion about just how many troths the widow plighted. She is believed to have contracted at least two successive marriages before, in the spring of 1950, she sneaked away from whatever spouse she then had and asked an American landing party to get her out of that complicated place. A year later, the remaining men on Anatahan agreed to surrender, conceivably because their last hope of marrying Kazuko was gone. By that time, there were only nineteen of them. It is generally accepted that some, if not all, of those who perished did so jousting for the love of the widow Higa—who, after her rescue, enjoyed a brief fling on the Tokyo night-club circuit, where she was billed as the Queen of Anatahan. A book of fiction called "Anatahan" was soon out, featuring a heroine who ran through a gamut of five island husbands; all of them were compared to Robinson Crusoe. Ultimately, Josef von Sternberg directed a Japanese movie version of "Anatahan," and at about the same time the island's Queen went back to her original home on Okinawa, where, to her surprise, she found her original husband. After what may have been a somewhat unsettling period of readjustment, the couple were cozily reunited.

During the first few postwar years, there was little the Japanese could do to entice their former soldiers out of distant nooks and crannies. To begin with, nobody could pinpoint the hideouts of any of these men, and a scattershot approach could hardly have done the trick. There are seven thousand islands in the Philippines alone, and in the vast oceanic area surrounding Guam, now called the Trust Territory of the Pacific Islands, there are some two thousand more. Then, in 1950, the Japanese had it on what seemed to be the fairly reliable authority of the nations administering the various regions of the western Pacific that not a single known straggler was left in any of them. Certainly, the administrators had done their best; the United States had saturated all the areas under its control with leaflets, had made broadcasts from ships and planes, had placed in conspicuous spots on some islands letters from the families of men who might be at large on those islands, and had sent out foot patrols. But the best wasn't very good—or, at any rate, it didn't work.

The Japanese Army had been so well indoctrinated against enemy propaganda that many of the soldiers in silent hiding refused to believe what they saw or heard. A photograph of the surrender ceremony aboard the battleship Missouri? Trick photography. A statement from the Emperor to the effect that Japan was at peace and they could return to it unharmed? Didn't sound like the Emperor *they* knew. Letters begging them to come home and assuring them that the Allied Occupation of Japan was humane, even gracious? Forgeries. Yuichi Akatsu hid out on the Philippine island of Lubang for five years. Back in the fall of 1945, he was on the point of giving himself up, in response to a leaflet that fluttered from the sky, when he examined the paper carefully. Aha! He spied what at first glance appeared to be a two-character Japanese word, "*kōfuku,*" meaning "surrender," which was what the Americans in the Philippines hoped that any Japanese reading the message would promptly and peaceably do. But an apostrophelike mark at the end of the second character was missing, and without that mark the word is meaningless. Akatsu was nobody's fool, and he concluded that the message had been written not by an authentic compatriot of his, who would surely never have made so obvious an error, but by some impostor. Why? Clearly, to dupe him into surrendering and thus exposing himself to consequences unimaginably appalling. Congratulating himself on his perspicacity, Akatsu ignored the message—which had in fact been composed, in perfectly good faith, if with some orthographical carelessness, by a Nisei in the American armed forces—and thus doomed himself to four additional years of misery. He ultimately got out of that bewildering area and back to his sense-making prewar occupation of fashioning children's hats.

Immediately after the war, the Japanese government was chiefly preoccupied with organizing and expediting the mass repatriation of large contingents of interned servicemen and assisting the families of the dead and missing. In 1948, several officials who had dealt with these matters were banded together in the Welfare Ministry's Repatriation Aid Bureau, under the Ministry of Health and Welfare, and Colonel Itagaki's subdivision of that bureau, the Repatriation Section, was made responsible for trying to find far-flung individual stragglers and help them to get home. Ever since this Section's founding, Itagaki has been assisted in running it by another retired Imperial Army officer, Major Yuzo Miura. Their office is in a drab and drafty wooden building, once a stable for cavalry horses, in a bureaucratic enclave in the Ichigaya district of Tokyo. More than thirty years ago, as student officers, Itagaki and Miura learned to ride at the same spot where they now seek sedentarily to corral stray comrades-at-arms. Their experiences over a dozen years have left them sharply cognizant of the danger of making any flat predictions about stragglers. Itagaki, who is as near to an authoritative government spokesman on straggling as any individual in Japan, thinks that there are probably no more stragglers anywhere, but he would not dream of omitting the "probably." And if by any chance there should still be some men at large, he points out, it might take some doing to catch up with them. "The longer you leave them out there, the cagier they get, and the more difficult it becomes to bring them back," Itagaki says.

4

EAT
OR BE EATEN

Of all the areas in which Japanese stragglers have roamed, New Guinea is generally considered the most forbidding. People can, and do, debate endlessly about the degree of disagreeableness of the world's many jungles. As a rule, the worst jungle is held to be the one that the man describing it has most recently been in. But among reasonably dispassionate folk who have visited several tropical zones it is conceded—once the conceder is back in civilization, and clean and dry and fed—that the jungles of New Guinea are a match for any. The Japanese had tens of thousands of soldiers in New Guinea during the war, and the Repatriation Section has seeded the area with a succession of enlightening leaflets. In 1954, the section tried to give aid and comfort to the distraught parents of a lone straggler who was thought to be in Papua—the southeastern part of New Guinea, which is under Australian jurisdiction. He was Ichiya Sugano, an Osaka man. His mother and father, who happened to be devout adherents of the Osaka Christian Mission, composed a message to him; the Repatriation Section had a hundred thousand copies of it printed, in Japanese and English; and arrangements were made to obtain the assistance of missionaries in Papua in distributing it. "ICHIYA come home very soon," the English version was headed, and the text said:

(1) The War closed nine years ago and officers and soldiers are back in their homes already and they are diligent in their own business.

(2) Come out ICHIYA very soon to the Missionary's house near you. Then you can go home. There is no fear, no danger. Never have suspicion about this.

(3) Through the Grace of God and the kindness of Missionaries in New Guinea we are very grateful to be able to drop the leaflets from the air.

But God's grace can be stymied by man. When the Repatriation Section is dealing with foreign nations, it must work through ordained diplomatic channels, and in this instance the leaflets it hoped to have dropped over New Guinea had to be dropped off first at the Japanese Embassy in Australia. That was as far as they got. They could not be moved from there without Australian sanction, and the Australians felt that it would be unfortunate to remind the New Guinea tribesmen of the possible continued presence of any Japanese. Ichiya never got his parents' plea, and he never came out—if, that is, he had ever gone in, and was still alive.

Four years after that, a Baptist missionary reported that while flying seventy-five miles from Hollandia, the capital of Netherlands New Guinea, he'd glimpsed five cabins in a cultivated area, with some untypically short men standing near them. This was in September of 1958, and by the time the Japanese government had made in-

quiry and received an answer through channels, it was
February of 1959. Then a reply came through the Dutch
Embassy in Tokyo, to the effect that a search of the
area in question had proved fruitless. The Dutch added,
almost with a sigh, "Time and time again rumors are
spread concerning the presence of Japanese soldiers in
Netherlands New Guinea." More such rumors were
spread just two months after that, in Tokyo, by a visiting
Dutch trader from Hollandia, who proclaimed his conviction that there were not a few but as many as five hundred *zanryūsha* still in the vicinity of his home town.

Since 1950, however, two groups of stragglers *have*
returned to Japan from New Guinea, and their utterly
dissimilar experiences illustrate how anarchy and order
can flourish almost side by side in the same environment.
The first batch of repatriates, consisting of eight infantry-
men, got home in mid-February of 1950, not long after
an Australian jungle patrol learned they were hanging
around some Papuan native settlements in the vicinity
of Madang. Despite the misgivings later expressed by the
Australians in the case of Ichiya, the Papuans were, by
and large, friendlier to outsiders than most Pacific Islanders. One Japanese soldier, Nobuo Wakabayashi, who
is now a retail clothing salesman in Okayama, in south
central Japan, was wounded by an American hand grenade and left for dead by his Japanese buddies; a native
chief came upon him, carried him to his village, and
spent nearly a year nursing him back to health. But however cordial the natives around Madang may have been,
if they had any notion that the war was over they either
could not or would not convey this news to the Japanese

they met. Of the eight New Guinea stragglers who reached home in 1950, not one knew what was what until the Australians grabbed him. One of the octet, a Fukuoka farmer named Yukimori Tsuda, spent a good deal of time with some natives who had been converted to Christianity, but although he picked up some spiritual knowledge from them, he got no temporal information. However, his recollections are by his own admission imprecise; he is the only straggler who has frankly acknowledged that his experiences temporarily addled him.

Perhaps the most unusual of these eight returnees is a frail and exceedingly lachrymose man named Minoru Noda. Now thirty-nine and a shipbuilder in the teeming port of Kobe, Noda was one of nine children in a farming family in Nagasaki Prefecture. In 1941, when he was nineteen, he enlisted in the Army and was sent for training to Korea, where he had a taxing and tearful time. People would keep hitting him, and he kept crying. Whenever the officers treated him decently, the noncommissioned officers would slap him around and make him cry. Whenever the N.C.O.s let up on him, the officers would start in, and he would cry some more. It was hardly a promising start for a soldier who was to survive six years on New Guinea. Moreover, during this training period, his health was poor, and he had a hard time keeping up with the older and stronger men. But after almost two years in Korea he regarded himself as a real soldier, ready to handle raw recruits in the conventional hard-fisted manner. When orders came through early in 1943 for his regiment to move out toward combat, however, the Army doctors said he was not physically fit to go along. Noda, like the other men in his unit, had already written his will and sent home a few snips of hair and some fingernail parings, in case he never got back whole. He begged his leaders to take him with them, and they countermanded the doctors' orders. With a thousand-stitched *sennimbari* wrapped snugly around his stomach, Noda set sail eagerly from Pusan. As his troopship steamed southeast, he would go up on deck every night, face in the direction of Japan, kneel down, pray, and shed copious tears.

Noda's unit spent a month on the island of Palau, practicing amphibious landings, boning up on jungle-fighting tactics, and gorging on fresh fish and fresh eggs. Then the soldiers moved on to New Guinea, landing in March at Hansa Bay, between Wewak and Madang on the northeast coast. En route, their ship barely escaped being torpedoed, and when they arrived, they were bombed and strafed as they were unloading. For a while, the men were put to work constructing roads and airfields, but then they were ordered to the Japanese front lines, which were rapidly crumbling as the Allies pressed farther and farther up the coast from the southeast. Noda, having come down with malaria almost at once, never actually got to do much fighting. At one point, he did find himself in charge of a light-machine-gun squad, but when he ran out of ammunition and saw little prospect of getting any more, he buried the weapon. Toward the end of 1943, after wandering around the seashore areas for many weeks, the men he was with had their previous ration of a yam a day reduced to a yam every three days. All were feverish, all were hungry, all were discouraged. According to Noda's highly emotional account, he had a somnambulistic dream in which he rose from his sleeping place, walked along a beautifully paved street, stopped to watch a circus put on by midgets, and dropped in at a public bath, where he was treated to a feast of all the boiled yams he could eat. When he awoke, he was in a deserted native hut, still famished. Not long after that, he and several other ailing men decided to head inland and take a chance on finding some food. They were disappointed, and for the next four or five months they kept alive by becoming cannibals.

Noda says he first tasted human flesh unwittingly. He met up with an amiable native who offered to trade him some fresh pork for a bit of dried ginger and a few cigarettes he had. After the swap, he was told by another native that his pork was human meat. Soon after that, he and the handful of men with him found the bodies of several Japanese soldiers, and cooked and ate the meat. They all got stomach pains, and Noda was horribly afflicted with hives—which may ultimately have saved his life. They made it impossible for him to abide the touch of clothing, and as he hobbled about in inflamed nakedness, he cut so unappetizing a figure that when his comrades ran out of meat again and began stalking each other, nobody cared much for the idea of eating him. Only one overt attempt was made on his life, he says, and this, ironically, by a man whom he himself had earlier saved from a cannibalistic assault. Upon being told by a confidant that the ungrateful man was going to kill and eat him, Noda sternly informed his potential aggressor that he knew about his intentions, and made him apologize.

"That interlude of cannibalism was the most horrible period of my life," Noda has since said, with genuine contrition. The men around him were so completely disorganized that the harsh sense of discipline beaten into them in their training days had all but vanished. The Japanese soldiers had a do-or-die saying, tied in with their Bushido code, that can be translated roughly as "Eat or be eaten." Now they were following it literally. Some of them warningly reminded their comrades of an old superstition that prolonged addiction to cannibalism can make a man's eyebrows rise, like Satan's, but this devillish prospect was no deterrent. One day, a lieutenant and a sergeant wandered out of the bush. Noda decided to receive them hospitably; he was unarmed, and both the newcomers had sabres, so he hoped his geniality would stand him in good stead if they were as hungry as he was. Accordingly, he made a big to-do about carrying their belongings into a native hut and finding them a corner to bed down in. But he failed to consider the possibility that the two late arrivals had not retrogressed as much in matters of military discipline as the men he'd been living with. He still had some cigarettes, and he offered each of the arrivals one, which they gratefully accepted, but then he made the mistake of lighting his own first. He was only a corporal, and the sergeant, incensed at this effrontery, threatened to chop his head off. "I dropped to my knees and bowed my head to the ground and apologized," Noda says. "But I suspected they wanted to kill me anyway, and I was right. That night, we overheard the lieutenant and the sergeant whispering; they were arguing about which of us to kill first. One of the men with me still had a gun, and we discussed the matter, and decided that if it was a matter of eat or be eaten with these two, we had better kill them first—as soon as they fell asleep. We agreed to chop off the sergeant's head with his own sword and to shoot the lieutenant. Because we thought he was a bad officer, we resolved to eat him quickly. We ate him, from head to toe, in three days."

After a while, they ran out of food once more, and the man with the gun came to Noda one night and asked who the next victim should be. Once they had made their choice, they agreed that they would toss a tent over the selectee while he was sleeping, and shoot him through the canvas. "When we threw the tent over him, he woke up," Noda recalls. "He sensed what we were up to and let out a muffled yell. 'You can't shoot me!' he cried. 'I have a mother waiting for me! I've got to get back to Japan!' He added that if we ate him, his soul would haunt us. The man with the gun pulled the trigger, and his weapon misfired. The second time, it worked. There was a shriek of 'Mother!' and our comrade was dead. Some of the others cooked him. Only four or five hours later, the man with the gun was felled with a terrible attack of malaria. The others at once killed *him*. I realized then how horrible a soul's revenge could be. I wondered what could save me. The Americans were pursuing us with all their weapons, some of the natives were after us with poisoned arrows, and meanwhile we Japanese were eating other Japanese. It got so bad that one day a close friend

of mine came to me and said, 'Please kill me and eat me.'
I scolded him and hit him in the face and told him to
stop that kind of talk. While I was wondering what
would happen next, I had a vision. I saw my mother's
face. She was a very religious woman, and she was praying for me. I told this to two men who were with me at
the time, and we all realized we shouldn't have been living the way we had, and we dropped to our knees and
prayed and cried. Then we went to a village where we'd
heard the inhabitants were friendly, and we knelt there
and prayed for thirty minutes with our eyes closed. When
we opened them, there were natives standing around us.
They looked at the meat we were carrying and said, 'Put
that away and eat the food Christ gave us.' They handed
us bananas and papayas and yams. I never ate human
meat again."

The natives next escorted the three Japanese to another village, called Gufu, whose residents, although they
were Christians, believed that when they died they would
be reincarnated with light skins. The elderly chief of
Gufu and his wife had lost their only son, a young man
named Lingali, not long before, and when Noda appeared, the bereaved mother pounced on him with cries
of "Lingali! Lingali!" For the next five years or so, Noda
lived as Lingali. Since by no means all the natives in that
region were so kindly disposed toward Japanese, Noda's
new relatives built him a hut in the jungle five miles from
their village, and they regularly trooped out to the hut
laden with food: a basic diet of yams, livened up with
delicacies his adoptive mother would press upon him—
plump lizards or rats, tasty bugs, occasionally a dog or a

cat. Mostly he lived alone, but from time to time other stragglers, who had been hiding outside other villages, would stop by and join him for a few weeks or months. He made frequent visits to Gufu to attend religious services, and he became so conversant with the local dialect that he began to preach sermons in it. "One day, when I had been there about three years, some of the natives, who believed that Christ's treasures were buried where their dead were buried, asked me if I could disclose these riches to them," Noda says. "A couple of other Japanese were staying with me at the time, and they said I was crazy to get mixed up in it, but I said I'd try, and I led some of the native priests to their cemetery. I told them that if we prayed and fasted there for ten days we might have a revelation. As the tenth day dawned, we were sitting around a fire, and while I was talking to a priest a toad suddenly jumped onto my knee. Next, it hopped onto my head, and from there to the priest's head and *his* knee. Then it plopped into the fire. I told the priest that the toad was Christ, and that by leaping into the fire He was showing them that He was still suffering and they hadn't yet prayed hard enough to get any reward. From then on, they went to church almost daily, and for a while they treated me almost like a god."

The chief of Gufu hoped that his pale-faced adoptive son would live there forever, would succeed him as the village headman, and, to perpetuate his line, would take a bride from the next village. Negotiations were initiated with the father of a girl deemed suitable for a chief presumptive, and for a time all proceeded in good order. Whiling away the days before his wedding, Noda raised yams, bananas, and sugar cane on a small farm. When his friends the natives came to call, he and they would all sit around congenially singing songs and eating frogs, which he caught at a nearby river when the moon was full. He also had a set of rattraps that he tended, to further vary his diet. He had given up all hope of ever leaving the environs of Gufu, which was twelve days' march from the coast, and he had lost all track of time. "I had even forgotten my own age," he says. "I was so intent on becoming a perfect native that if it hadn't been for the Japanese soldiers who occasionally visited me I'd probably have forgotten our language." Then, suddenly, the chief and his wife both took sick and died. After a night spent weeping over their bodies, Noda helped carry them to the graveyard, at dawn, and bury them. With their demise, the marriage negotiations abruptly stopped, and the orphaned Noda was left pretty much on his own.

A few weeks afterward, a pair of stragglers living in the next village, who had been hailed by *their* native neighbors as nothing more exciting than a pair of stragglers, got bored with their humdrum lot and made the twelve-day trek to the seashore, where they were grabbed by a roving Australian patrol. The Japanese confessed to their captors that there were other stragglers inland, and the Australians headed toward Gufu. As word of their arrival reached the village, a courier raced to Noda's hut with the upsetting news. Three other stragglers—Haruo Tominaga, Toru Yamamoto, and Yoshinobu Miura—were sharing his quarters at the moment. Tominaga, who was ill, was delighted to hear that deliverance was near, but the other men were afraid that the Australians would kill them, and they seriously considered suicide. They decided finally to take a chance, and walked to Gufu to surrender. "It wasn't easy for me to leave my little farm and my rattraps and the rivers and mountains," Noda says, "but, crying, I walked to the village. I stopped to pray at the graves of my parents. In the village, nearly five hundred natives gathered around me to say farewell. I couldn't say much in response; I was crying too hard."

Several months after that, Noda was back in Nagasaki. By this time, he had developed such a severe case of malaria that he had to spend most of the next three years in a hospital. Following his release, in 1953, he married a local girl. Then, after a fling at selling insurance and working in a cannery, he moved to Kobe, where he now lives, with his wife and their two children—a girl of seven and a boy of five—in a one-room, unheated apartment, and works in a shipyard a short walk away. The apartment, measuring approximately eight feet by twelve, is furnished with an old-fashioned washing machine, an umbrella, and a television set. Some evenings, Noda's wife and a friend or two sit with him on the tatami-covered floor, sipping green tea, and listening as he reminisces tearfully about his strange cannibalistic days and his life as Lingali, while his two children, oblivious of his narrative, huddle before the TV set, watching an American Western with dubbed-in Japanese dialogue.

In striking contrast to the behavior of Noda and the stragglers who returned with him in 1950 was that of four Japanese soldiers—the scrawny, sick survivors of a group of sixteen—who were taken off New Guinea in September of 1954. They, too, had entertained thoughts of cannibalism, but had reached a conclusion that one of them, Mamoru Ojima, has summed up as "I'd starve to death before I'd eat human meat." Ojima, a former corporal from Tsuyama, a town outside Okayama, almost did starve in the jungle, more than once, and on his return to Japan he had to spend ten months in the hospital for malaria and malnutrition. In a report on this quartet of stragglers, the Repatriation Section, which does not normally go in for fancy prose, made the observation "The fact is that these four men were all great men. They didn't care about themselves selfishly. They were always concerned with group survival, and they comforted and consoled each other. They were almost like gods."

The first word anybody in Japan had that these near-immortals were still definitely among the mortals came in October, 1954. That month, a letter from Mamoru Ojima—who, according to official Japanese records, had died at Aitape, New Guinea, on April 25, 1944—was received by his older brother, a farmer in Okayama Prefecture. Ojima, in Hollandia, had also written to his father, but that letter went undelivered; his father had been dead for seven years. His letter to his brother was laconic. "I left for Hollandia in April, 1944," he wrote, "but through landing operations of the U.S. Army could not proceed and stayed in the jungle for ten years, and was recently found by the Dutch authorities and taken care of. The man in charge has told me I'll be sent home by ship or air in two or three months. Four men have been taken care of, including me, and one is the son of Shimada."

The son of Shimada, a casual acquaintance of the Ojima family, was Kakuo Shimada, a master sergeant and the highest-ranking soldier in this new-found group. The two other men, whom Ojima did not identify in his terse letter, were Sanzo Yaegashi, of Iwate Prefecture, in northern Japan, and Kumao Shimokubo, of Miyazaki Prefecture, far to the south. A day or two after Ojima's family received their tidings, Shimokubo's father got a similar, though much more detailed, message. (Concurrently, the Dutch government was notifying the Japanese government about the four men, but news does not always flow as fast through diplomatic channels as by airmail.) Shimokubo went on at some length about the date and place of his enlistment in the Army—which could hardly have been news to his father—and added:

There is something I can't express in words when I think of my father and mother, who must be reading this letter about a son who has supposedly been dead for ten years, and when I think about myself. I just can't write, and the only thing I can do is look at the desk and do nothing. I can't set down all my troubles and agonies, so I think I'd better keep them inside me until I meet you, in several months. . . . My feelings are so complicated I can't make up my mind right now whether to come home or to stay here until I die. The Dutch have been urging us to go back to Japan, but after spending so long a time on this island, it might be hard for me to find a way to live in Japan, arriving there empty-handed. Although there is so much I'd like to write, my mixed-

up feelings keep me from writing. I will put my pen on
the desk now, and I'll be looking forward to seeing you,
sir.

Shimada, Ojima, Shimokubo, and Yaegashi were
members of the 209th Airfield Squadron, which did
ground maintenance for a light-bomber unit in Manchuria early in the war and then was shipped southeast,
arriving at Wewak, on the north coast of New Guinea,
in November, 1943. It had been scheduled to train recruits in maintenance work there, but by the time it
arrived the Japanese military position had become so
shaky and Allied air raids so effective that there were
scarcely any planes to maintain. Soon there were none
at all, and early in April of 1944, for want of anything
more constructive to do, ninety officers and men in the
outfit decided to hike northwest along the coast toward
Hollandia, more than three hundred miles away. There
the Japanese Army had a big and well-fortified supply
base, and the maintenance men believed it to be an
oasis of power and plenty—a belief that was shared by
other Japanese in the region, who were also moving
northwest under the mounting Allied pressure. The men
from the 209th figured it would take them about thirty
days to march to Hollandia, and each carried a month's
rations—mostly rice, dried vegetables, and bean paste.
They did not know that just as they were starting off for
Hollandia, so was a large Allied amphibious assault
force. The American I Corps hit Hollandia on April
22nd, and other Allied troops were already pushing up
the coast behind the Japanese. "We were rats in a sack,"

Shimada has since said. "But, of course, we weren't aware of that back then, so we kept on moving. We figured we were bound to find *something* in Hollandia when we got there." Few of them ever got close. Enemy bullets and bombs, malaria, and general debilitation thinned their ranks swiftly. Seven or eight men were lost when the troops tried to cross a turbulent coastal river on improvised rafts. Others simply disappeared. In less than a month, only Shimada and eight companions remained of the ninety men who had set forth. Since he was the highest-ranking of the bunch, he took charge.

The quality of leadership is hard to define, in or out of battle. Some men simply have it, and Shimada, like Corporal Kishi on Morotai, was one of them. Shimada does not look or act especially masterful. He is physically unprepossessing—pale and square-faced—and he speaks in a soft voice. In 1944, he was twenty-four, a farm boy from Kamiukan, a rural settlement in central Japan, fifteen miles north of the village of Takahashi, where he lives today. Civilian life had afforded him scant opportunity to give commands or assume responsibilities. He had joined the Army at twenty-one, but had not been much tempered in the fire of battle. Yet in New Guinea he demonstrated exceptional fitness for transforming potentially thorny situations into reasonably smooth ones. An instance of this occurred in 1946, when his group, reduced to five half-starved and ailing men, retrieved a cache of salt they had hidden a year or so before. It amounted to only a couple of pounds, but this represented a real treasure. Today, most of the stragglers recall their yearning for salt as more overwhelming and passionate than any sexual cravings they had. While skulking in the inland hills, Shimada's men had risked capture time and again by making trips to the shore, hauling back sea water, and boiling it or letting it evaporate until it yielded a cherished residue of salt. (Ito and Minagawa, who performed a similar operation on Guam, have estimated that in a year they were able to refine about half a peck of salt from half a ton of sea water.) When the group found its precious two pounds of salt, Shimada gathered his men around him and announced that he expected the salt to last them at least ten years. He poured a trickle into each man's hand, to illustrate what a year's individual ration would amount to, and then consigned the precious stuff to a communal box, decreeing that it was to be opened and its contents doled out only on New Year's Day, the Emperor's Birthday, and other festive occasions. Shimada is not the kind of Japanese who, invested with the authority of superior rank, would have chopped off a subordinate's head, or even cuffed him, for arguing against such a rigid program, but nobody disputed his decision. "I wanted to make that salt last as long as I could," he says. "The lack of it makes men impatient, and, much as we needed salt, we needed patience more."

Back in 1944, Shimada's original eight men were joined in their march toward Hollandia by seven others, who had become separated from their units. Allied patrols, trying to wipe out all the rats in the sack, were scouring the coastal trails with increasing diligence, and Shimada's men were too weak to move fast or far; for one harrowing forty-eight-hour stretch they slogged through a swamp so deep that there was no place a man could even sit down. To avoid the American patrols and find a place for his men to rest, Shimada decided to strike inland and to hide out temporarily in the jungle a couple of miles from a Japanese supply dump that the Allies had overrun. At night, he thought, his men might be able to sneak past the sentries at the dump and steal some provisions. "I had concluded that for every day we kept on marching one of my soldiers would probably collapse and die," Shimada says. "Anyway, we had heard by then that the Americans were in Hollandia, and it seemed foolish to get there before the Japanese had retaken the place, which none of us had the slightest doubt they would do within a month or two." For nearly a year, the stragglers lived in a crude shelter near the supply dump. From the latter they managed to obtain some clothes and enough food to get by on, but as the months passed, malaria and a few well-aimed bullets from American sentries killed off five of the sixteen.

The fifth of May is celebrated as Children's Day in Japan, and the survivors observed the holiday in 1945 by playing games most of the night, by the light of a small, flickering, and, they hoped, well-screened fire. With pieces they had carved, they engaged zestfully in round after round of Go, mah-jongg, and shogi, the Japanese version of chess. The next morning, they were tired and off their guard. When one of them announced that he had heard a twig snap, another suggested that it was probably just a wild boar or some other animal. Ojima was not sure. He went out to look around, and from a knoll above their hideout he saw enemy soldiers ad-

vancing. He yelled a warning, and his companions
tumbled out and took to the woods, with bullets singing
past them. Three were killed. Yaegashi got a flesh wound
in his thigh, but was still able to move. All this was bad
enough, but it was horrifying when the attacking patrol,
having chased the Japanese away, set fire to their shelter.
When the patrol was gone and the eight surviving stragglers reassembled, they discovered that just about everything they had possessed was in ashes. The next day,
they discovered that the Allies had also put the torch
to the supply depot on which they'd been so dependent.
The only food that hadn't been ruined was some dried
biscuit packed in cans. For the following year, that was
to be their chief sustenance. During this austere period,
three more men died.

Early in 1946, Shimada concluded that whenever
the Japanese Army might be coming back, it seemed
unlikely that it would be very soon, and that if he and
his four companions wanted to stay alive, they had better
start producing their own food. For weeks they searched
for a promising piece of land to till, and they finally
found one about thirty miles from the scorched dump.
The spot they picked was near a village called Koya,
which is a couple of days' walk inland from Hollandia,
Ojima had gone to an agricultural school as a boy, had
passed a national examination in farming techniques, and
before entering the Army had worked for his home prefecture as an agricultural adviser. Now he was a
theoretician become practitioner. He found some sweet-
potato vines, and these the men planted on an acre or so
that they had laboriously cleared with their sabres and

a few tools they had picked up in their wanderings—a hatchet, a scythe, and a saw. But what were they to eat until harvest time? They went back to the burned-out supply dump, picked up all the tinned hardtack they could find, and, in several burdensome trips, carted it to their new home. One can was supposed to provide one man with one meal. They figured that they had enough tins to last them for six months—on the basis of one can per man per day. The cache proved useful in another way. The biscuits were wrapped in a gauze-like material, and after a few months the stragglers accumulated enough of this to make some clothing, and also a mosquito net big enough to cover them all as they slept. After four months, their potato plants were lushly leafy, and the eager gardeners dug up their crop. To their dismay, the entire yield turned out to be about ten pounds of puny, thumb-sized potatoes. The biscuits by then were all but gone. Gamely, the Japanese at once planted a second potato crop, and also put in some banana sprouts they had found. While waiting appre-hensively for these plants to grow, they ate whatever they could find—wild fruits, frogs and lizards, worms and grasshoppers, the pulp of certain trees, and the broad leaves of their potato crop. The leaves gave them dysen-tery. But their second crop was a good one, and around the time it came in, their periodic forays into the sur-rounding forest netted them six rusty rifles—five of which they managed to coddle into working shape—and three hundred rounds of ammunition. But not until early 1948 did they dare go hunting; up to then, they were fearful of betraying their location with shots. After that,

they occasionally bagged a cassowary or a wild boar.
Once, after killing a wild sow, they captured her piglets,
which they put into a crude sty with the idea of breeding
them. But the shoats kept breaking out and rooting up
the vegetable garden, so they had to be slaughtered. In
1948, another man died of malaria. And then there were
four—Shimada, Ojima, Shimokubo, and Yaegashi.

As their diet gradually improved and their strength
increased, the four men began improving their living
conditions. In the early days at their farm, they had tried
to build a log cabin, but the effort of cutting a single
log had drained their energy, so they had merely sheltered themselves as best they could with slim boughs
and tenting. Now they were able to erect a fairly cozy
cabin, about thirty feet long and ten feet wide, which
they roofed and floored with broad palm fronds. They
dammed a nearby stream and used the resulting pool
for washing their clothes and bathing; downstream, they
set up a latrine. They made new clothes from tree fibres,
though they didn't require much in the way of garments;
mostly, they just wore loincloths. Their feet had long
since become so calloused that they had no need of
shoes.

But as their life became more tolerable, and they
had time to think about something besides mere survival,
boredom set in. There were few conversational topics
they had not exhausted. They had talked incessantly
about the food they would eat when, or if, they ever
got out of the jungle, and they had talked about their
families, and they had talked about their plight. "After
a while, we had nothing to talk about," Ojima recalls.

"We sometimes felt that the soldiers who had died were luckier than we were. Once or twice, after we found the rifles, we discussed the idea of going out and finding some enemy soldiers and attacking them, so they would kill us and end our misery. But that was really just talk; we never seriously wanted to bring about our own deaths. Nobody would kill himself unless he was crazy. Besides, we had been taught to commit suicide only if we were on the point of capture, and we seemed to be in no danger of *that*. And we were all determined that if the Japanese Army did come back to our part of New Guinea, we would rejoin it and fight again for our country."

Once, hoping to learn something of outside affairs, they walked to the seashore. They saw a flotilla of Allied ships off the coast, and concluded that the war was probably still going on somewhere beyond their limited earshot. They all agreed upon this conclusion; they hardly ever argued about anything. Now and then, one of them briefly became peeved at the others; in such instances it was their policy to ignore the dissenter until he cooled off. None of them, no matter how put out he might momentarily be, ever contemplated abandoning his comrades and striking off on his own, for they were all conscious of their interdependence. They had no particular religious convictions; coöperation was their binding faith. "What kind of a god would have condemned men to the kind of life we led?" one of the survivors has asked.

Master Sergeant Kakuo Shimada was unarguably in command, but although most Japanese military leaders insisted that in all circumstances their subordinates address them in respectful terms, he asked the others to stop calling him Sergeant and to call him Kak-san. Ojima, whose name is sometimes pronounced "Kojima," became Kojiko. Sanzo Yaegashi was San-chan, and Kumao Shimo-kubo was Kuma-san. Kak-san had acquired some skill at working metals during his hitch as a maintenance man in Manchuria. Now he made a forge and an anvil, and from metal objects that he collected in the jungle he fashioned a chisel and a plane, a razor and a pair of shears, and some eating utensils. Ojima, who in his pre-war agricultural stint had watched Japanese farmers make charcoal, proceeded to dig a charcoal pit. At best, how-ever, the four men were still leading a marginal existence. They knew now that they would not starve, but in nearly five years at their farm they had not laid eyes on another human being; indeed, they were completely in the dark as to whether the natives in the area were cordial or hostile.

In the summer of 1951, they found out. Yaegashi, who was setting out on a hunting expedition, saw some footprints that were too large to have been made by Jap-anese feet. He summoned his comrades, and they fol-lowed the tracks as far as they could. The next week, a dog came sniffing around their hut. Since they had never seen a wild dog in that region, they figured it must be a pet. Shimada, Ojima, and Shimokubo followed it, leav-ing Yaegashi, who had been laid low with malaria, at home with a loaded rifle. The three men pursued the dog for five hundred yards or so, in jungle so dense they couldn't see five feet ahead. Just as they were about to turn back, they heard a shout of "Japan, *ka?*" The

"Japan" was in English; "*ka*" in Japanese is an articulated question mark. They conferred hastily, and then Shimada called out, "*Hai*, Japan!" "*Hai*" is Japanese for "yes." The voice thereupon said, "*Mari, mari.*" "*Mari*" means "come" in Malay; the Japanese had learned the word years before, from Indonesian prisoners conscripted to work for their Army.

As Shimada, Ojima, and Shimokubo sought out the owner of the voice, they had a fleeting glimpse of some natives running off. As the natives ran, they kept calling "*Mari, mari,*" and the Japanese kept following them. At last, one native stopped behind a tree. The stragglers couldn't see whether or not he was armed. If this was an ambush, they wanted to make sure they wouldn't all be trapped by it, especially with Yaegashi alone and sick in the hut. So Ojima, a crack marksman, hung back, covering the others with a rifle. When Shimada and Shimokubo had come within ten yards of the native, he gestured to them to drop their rifles and ammunition sacks. They complied. Then the native stepped out and shook hands with them. Shimada yelled to Ojima to lay down his weapon and join them. By the time Ojima reached the group, two other natives had materialized.

The Japanese thought it would be tactful to give their new acquaintances some presents. Shimokubo ran back to the cabin and returned with three knives Shimada had made, and also a bunch of bananas, which the natives ate with every appearance of relish, though these could hardly have constituted much of a treat. They fingered the knives with awe, admiring the keenness of the blades. Meanwhile, all concerned tried to con-

verse. Shimada and Ojima, seeking military infoma-
tion, pantomimed rifle fire and said, in Japanese, "Japan?
America? Hollandia?" The natives looked blank. After
a few more abortive attempts to exchange intelligence,
two of the natives, whose names the stragglers later
learned were Laniel and Kamen, pointed to the sky and
made gestures, which the Japanese interpreted to mean
that the pair would come to call at their hut when the
sun had slept ten times.

For the next ten days the Japanese forwent hunting
and stuck close to home. They were still not certain of
the natives' intentions, and when the ten days had
passed and there was no sign of their new acquaintances,
they grew nervous. But on the twelfth day Laniel and
Kamen showed up. They inspected the stragglers' quarters minutely, and were particularly taken with Shimada's
smithy. The Sergeant noticed that the tips of some arrows the guests were carrying were worn and blunt, and
on the spot he fashioned a sharp new arrowhead for one
of them. The natives were enchanted with it. They also
had some dull-edged sabres with them, and Shimada
offered to sharpen these. Laniel and Kamen left the
swords with him, promising to come back and fetch them
after three more sunsets. This time, they arrived on
schedule, and brought along a delegation of eight other
tribesmen from their home village—it was Koya—including their chief, a man named Faloan. They also
brought a bundle of arrows and sabres that needed re-
pairs. Koya was a whole day's walk from the stragglers'
retreat, but after that some of the natives came to see the
Japanese frequently. At the start, communication wasn't

easy. The stragglers learned, however, that the natives had known of their whereabouts for two years or so, having heard them shooting game. It had taken the Koya men seven hundred suns to muster up enough nerve to approach within hailing distance. Now that they were all friends, the natives brought seeds that the Japanese could plant to vary their diet—peanuts and pumpkins, eggplant and sugar cane, and, best of all, cayenne pepper, to add some piquancy to their bland fare. The natives also brought tobacco, which the stragglers wrapped in banana leaves, to make the first cigarettes they'd had for ages; at night, when the visitors had left, they played mah-jongg, using the roll-your-owns as prizes. There were no coconut trees within walking distance of the Japanese farm, so the natives brought coconuts. They also brought a ragged copy of *Life*, four or five years old. None of the Japanese knew any English, but the issue carried a picture of an American walking jauntily past the grounds of the Imperial Palace, in Tokyo. This was the most persuasive evidence the stragglers had yet come upon that maybe the war wasn't progressing according to Imperial plan. (At just about the time they saw the magazine, the six-year American Occupation of Japan was drawing to a close.) The natives themselves professed to be utterly ignorant of international affairs, and the Japanese agreed that the only safe thing to do was to stay where they were—especially since the natives were now making their existence a good deal more bearable. Faloan and his tribesmen taught them how to hunt with bows and arrows, and showed them jungle grasses from which medicines could be brewed. All four of the Japanese had been chronically sick, but Yaegashi was the frailest among them, and he found this pharmacological guidance especially welcome. He had been flat on his back with malaria or some other illness as often as he'd been up and about; every now and then his companions had tugged him to his feet and forced him to walk around, lest his muscles atrophy from disuse. The Koya men taught the Japanese their words for many objects, and the stragglers carefully wrote these down, phonetically, on strips of bark with pieces of Ojima's charcoal. Hunting had become a fairly sedentary pursuit for the Japanese, who, because of their diminished strength, would usually rig up a blind and sit in it until some game came their way. Now, as they waited, they practiced the native words they'd learned. One day, when their friends from Koya took them fishing, they met some people from another village, whom the Koya men addressed in a tongue unfamiliar to the Japanese. This was a language that was more widespread in New Guinea than the local dialect, and the name of it, as they recall, was Toan. Soon the Japanese were boning up on Toan, and in the years since they've been home Shimada and Ojima have amused themselves by occasionally corresponding in a phonetic version of that language.

It was thanks to the natives that the stragglers were ultimately repatriated. The Japanese never learned exactly how this came about, but by this time they have pieced together a fairly complete explanation. Faloan, the chief, had a bad leg, so he turned over his post to a son. The son's wife was the daughter of a native policeman with connections in Hollandia, and she confided to her father that the Koya villagers were succoring a group of Japanese. Presently she died, and her father suspected that she'd been poisoned by the Koya tribesmen. Vengefully hoping to get them in trouble—or so the Japanese were led to believe—he tipped off the local Dutch authorities to the presence of the stragglers. It is difficult to understand how the natives could, on the one hand, have had such relatively easy access to government authorities and, on the other, have been so uninformed about outside events. However this may have been, the Dutch did find out about the Japanese, and sent an armed patrol to round them up. The stragglers surrendered without resistance on being told that the war was over, and that the Emperor was in good health, and that Japan and the United States were at peace. "Also we came out for the reason that we couldn't have continued our accustomed way of life much longer," Shimada said on reaching Japan. "White ants were destroying our house."

All four men were ill for quite a while after arriving home, in the fall of 1954. Shimokubo—who was married early in 1959, now has a son, and works in a machine foundry near Nagasaki—had a spot on one lung. "Because of all the jungle diseases, my strength isn't as good as that of ordinary men," he said not long ago. It is hardly surprising that he should regard himself as extraordinary. Yaegashi is dead. His home was in one of the most frigid sections of Japan, and his wasted body couldn't adjust to an environment so frostily different from that of the tropics. He got married in 1956, and had two children, but his health gradually declined, and he died on November 24, 1960, at the age of forty-one. His death was a blow to Shimada and Ojima; they had planned to visit him the following month. The three of them had had one reunion earlier that year (Shimokubo hadn't been able to make it), and had had a merry time exchanging reminiscences, some of them in Toan. Shimada and Ojima feel that Yaegashi's death came about in part because, though physically he was no match for his three companions, he had always insisted on doing his full quarter share of their joint chores whenever he was able to move under his own power.

Shimada currently works as a supervisor in a Takahashi factory that makes picture frames, decorative boxes, and other objects of carved wood. He got married the year after his homecoming, to a woman who runs a beauty parlor, and they have a four-year-old daughter. Ojima got married at just about the same time, and has a daughter a month younger than Shimada's. Ojima is a clerk in the head office of a company that operates an inn, a children's-wear store, and a *pachinko*—pinball— parlor. "I guess maybe I am a more understanding man than I might have been if I hadn't stayed in New Guinea all that time," he says, "but I sometimes think that it was a terrible disadvantage for me to have spent the best years of my life in the jungle. The world changed too fast for me. I think I was sort of left behind."

5

NAKED
TO EACH OTHER

On December 19, 1944, while General MacArthur's forces were poised to make a landing at Lingayen Gulf, on the island of Luzon, and begin the final phase of the reconquest of the Philippines, two young Japanese Army second lieutenants, Hiroo Onoda and Shigeichi Yamamoto, boarded a light bomber in Tokyo and were flown to Clark Field, outside Manila. Both officers were from Wakayama Prefecture, southwest of Tokyo, and both had recently graduated from an Imperial Army course in guerrilla and sabotage techniques. Upon reaching the Philippines, the two men almost at once went their separate ways, and they never saw each other again, but they were fated to enjoy a common celebrity.

Both Yamamoto and Onoda had thankless tasks assigned to them. By mid-December, it was all but inevitable that MacArthur would soon retake the Philippines, and just four days before the lieutenants left their homeland, an Allied amphibious force, undeterred by cruel punishment from kamikaze planes, had gone ashore on the island of Mindoro, a hundred miles south of Manila. Mindoro itself was not a major Allied objective, but San Jose, at its southeast corner, had been selected as a fine spot to base American fighter aircraft supporting the invasion of Luzon. Yamamoto had been given command of an outfit, a couple of hundred men strong, whose job it was to wreck, or at least damage, the landing strips and other facilities that Allied engineers had feverishly begun constructing. Yamamoto and his men were supposed to slip silently into the San Jose base, surprise its garrison, preferably at knife point, and dynamite its installations. Even if they succeeded, their chances of getting away alive were slim; the two hundred were, in effect, walking kamikazes. If they should be detected before they could plant their explosive charges, they were to make a frontal attack, and for such a banzai assault Yamamoto had been issued a broad white sash, which he was to don as he led his men to annihilation. Onoda, for his part, had been sent to the little island of Lubang, just off the northwest tip of Mindoro, and his orders were to prevent Allied use of an airstrip that the Japanese had previously carved out there. He reached Lubang on December 31, 1944, and, in the opinion of some of the residents of that island, he may still be there today.

Mindoro, with an area of thirty-seven hundred square miles, is the seventh largest of the seven thousand islands that make up the Philippines. Most of Mindoro's inhabitants, who number slightly over a hundred thousand, live along the coast, are fairly civilized, and are Christians. Because of the island's mountainous topography, there are no direct communications between the east and west coasts, and practically no roads, and in the largely inaccessible interior dwell some twenty thousand pagan aborigines, whose ancestors emigrated from the mainland of Southeast Asia. The aborigines are known collectively as Mangyans, which means "hill people" in Tagalog, but in fact there are at least eight distinct tribes of Mangyans, each with its own customs and language. The one trait that most Mangyans share is an astonishing primitiveness. They seldom stray from their tribal preserves; a seventy-year-old man who has spent his whole life within sight of the sea does not regard it as strange that he has never traversed the few miles that separate him from the shoreline. The Mangyans are rarely visited by outlanders. Occasionally, a missionary or an anthropologist will drop in, or, even less frequently, a prospector, bolstered by the hope that Mindoro will someday live up to its alluring name, which is derived from "*mina de oro*," the Spanish for "gold mine;" legend has it that the place is a repository of vast mineral resources. If these exist, practically none have even been tapped, and over the years the island has been celebrated mainly for a trio of features; its Mangyans, its extremely high incidence of malaria, and its timarau—a breed of animal, now nearly extinct, that looks like a cross between a deer and a carabao, or water buffalo. The aborigines are not especially fierce. As far as is known, none of the Mangyan tribes go in for either head-hunting or cannibalism. During the war, almost all of them, it is believed, became terrified of the Japanese. Mindoro was not heavily garrisoned while Japan occupied the Philippines, but enough Japanese spent enough time in its interior for reports to circulate over the hill people's grapevine that anybody unfortunate enough to fall into the intruders' clutches would probably have his nose or his ears sliced off. Accordingly, the natives were not apt to be charitably disposed toward any Japanese who fell into their clutches.

It was across part of the Mangyans' forbidding and inhospitable terrain that Yamamoto and his fellow-saboteurs resolutely marched, having been put ashore east of San Jose. They got close to their destination, but they had no chance either to sneak up on the base quietly or, with the lieutenant draped in his ceremonial sash, to charge in clamorously. Outside San Jose, the night they arrived, the sky was suddenly lit up with lurid flares. In the glare, Allied troops opened up with withering fire, and the little band of infiltrators was chopped down. It was an experience dismayingly familiar to Japanese on many battlefields in the Philippines; of some six hundred and thirty thousand Imperial Army soldiers on the islands, four hundred and seventy-five thousand were killed in the course of MacArthur's emphatic return.

Yamamoto and thirty enlisted men survived the abortive raid, and, like other Japanese soldiers reeling from other routs in other Pacific combat zones, they found themselves wandering around in the jungle, hungry, sick, scared, bewildered, and helpless, but not hopeless. They, too, were convinced that sooner or later their Emperor would send someone to get them out of their fix. Like many of the other *zanryūsha*, Yamamoto and his men were, in the course of their travels, to happen upon Allied leaflets informing them that the war was over, that Japan's military sun had set, and that they should surrender; but, like other stragglers, Yamamoto,

who had been taught that the enemy was capable of all
sorts of underhanded tricks, dismissed such importunities
as hokum. Besides, for many months after the first of the
leaflets appeared, there was evidence annoyingly close
at hand that hostilities had not ceased. Filipino guerrilla
units were ranging the hills, eager to wipe out any Japanese
pockets of resistance that might remain, and some of the
Mangyans had been issued weapons and invited to assist.
In their first year or so on Mindoro, Yamamoto's band engaged in no fewer than eight skirmishes with these guerrilla
bands. The lieutenant was wounded four times—once
by a rifle bullet, the other times by grenades. One of the
oldest men in his party, Seiji Izumida, the man who was
to find a mysterious box under his tombstone, was shot
in the leg during one of these encounters. Izumida, a
farmer from Nagasaki Prefecture, couldn't walk for three
months. On being wounded, he felt he would be an
intolerable burden and besought Yamamoto to kill him.
But Yamamoto refused, pointing out that Izumida had
a wife and two sons at home. The stragglers by then
had no medical supplies, but the lieutenant improvised
a bandage out of softened tree bark and directed that
the wounded man be carried by his companions, and
Izumida pulled through. Not all those wounded were as
lucky; most of the soldiers were before long in such
weakened condition that superficial injuries proved fatal.
By the end of 1945, only fifteen of the original thirty
men in the contingent were alive.

Yamamoto feared that they would all perish if they
kept on drifting. Their only hope, he told them, lay in
establishing a permanent base and growing some crops.

The Filipino guerrillas, in the tradition of Mindoro, were sticking fairly close to the coast, so Yamamoto led his men far inland. Fifteen men, he then declared, would be too many for a single commune. He left seven of them on an arable mountain slope and, with the remaining seven, moved two days' march away, to the top of a thirty-six-hundred-foot hill called Mount Ayamitan. The eight stragglers appropriated a handy cave, and, with their foot-and-a-half-long sabres, plus a single axe, their only proper tool, began clearing a half-acre patch of soil. The next need was for something to plant. Scouting the area around their site, the Japanese found a village of natives a half-hour's walk distant. The stragglers warily approached the natives—who, it seems from available anthropological information, were probably members of a Mangyan tribe called the Buhid—and, to their relief, were greeted without rancor. Soon the stragglers were swapping some of their meagre possessions for sweet potatoes and corn, which were to become their staple foods, and also for some chickens and pigs. A pair of Army underdrawers got them a sow. Several of the stragglers had wristwatches, and the natives were curious about these, and fascinated by the ticking. A watch strap or watch case fetched merely a couple of handfuls of seed, but the inner works were good for a hen. (When the works stopped ticking, the natives disassembled them and used the gears as earrings.) In May, 1946, the stragglers were ready to plant, and in September, after a lean interval during which they lived mostly on wild fruits and vegetables, it was harvest time. The first crop was a bumper one. "Our happiness when we ate this food was

the high point of all the years we spent on Mindoro,"
Yamamoto has said.

Heartened and strengthened, the men built a log
hut. Behind it they constructed a *yasukuni*, a shrine
memorializing their fallen comrades-in-arms, and having
been informed by the Buhid in sign language of a few
native beliefs, also deferentially put up a shrine honoring
the god of Mount Ayamitan. They placed in the *yasukuni* some hair and fingernail parings they had taken
from the bodies of their companions who had died, and
every morning and every evening they took an offering
of sweet potatoes to the hallowed spot. By the beginning
of 1947, they were so well off that they were able to throw
a lively New Year's party. They butchered a male pig
(a sow and some piglets were snoozing promisingly nearby), made a ceremonial offering of its head, and feasted
on roast pork. Then they sang their national anthem, the
"Kimigayo," and other songs—among them one composed
for the occasion by Shigehira Nakano, who in civilian
life had been a barber in Iwate Prefecture, in northeast
Japan. It was a martial air called "On the Way to Mindoro." Next, they held a storytelling contest, and a soldier
named Yamada, whose entry was a tender and passionate
reverie about his girl friend, was unanimously adjudged
the winner.

Not long after Yamamoto and his men had begun
trafficking with the natives, an exhausted Japanese soldier
stumbled into their compound. He was one of the seven
members of their earlier contingent they'd left behind on
the other mountainside—the only one, he reported sadly,
to have survived a raid by some Mangyans they had

previously looked upon as docile. Yamamoto concluded that it would be prudent to have as little truck as possible with any natives thenceforth—even the ostensibly gentle Buhid people. He cautioned his men to stay alert day and night, and, wherever they were and whatever they were doing, to be ready for instant action. Since they had little need for clothing in the blistering climate, they generally went about only in loincloths, but each man always wore a belt from which hung a woven-grass pouch containing two hand grenades.

Little by little, the group cleared additional land— about half an acre a year. Corn and sweet potatoes remained the principal crops, but, as time went on, the Japanese came upon other plants and seeds, and soon they were cultivating sugar cane, pineapples, bananas, tobacco, onions, garlic, ginger, and pepper. These last were especially welcome, for the men had absolutely no salt, and now they could at least give some zest to their fare. They ate twice a day, as a rule—potatoes being their staple for breakfast, corn for dinner. At first they concocted side dishes out of rats, snakes, lizards, snails, and monkeys (the monkey skins they used for blankets), but after about a year, so rapidly had their livestock multiplied, they were able to substitute pork and fowl. Later, they had seventy chickens and twenty pigs.

Before long, the men built a bigger and more comfortable house, which had sleeping rooms, a living room, rattan floor mats, a bathtub, a veranda furnished with armchairs, and a kitchen with a clay oven and running water, piped in from an upland stream through bamboo tubes. Nakano, the songwriting barber, had managed to hang on to his scissors and a razor, and he gave his mates haircuts and shaves. Contraptions were fashioned for grinding corn and mashing potatoes. Izumida, by now recovered from his leg wound, began fooling around with mashed bananas, and produced some home brew. He started modestly, with canteen-size lots, but his product had such an uplifting effect on his comrades that he soon switched to a one-and-a-half-gallon jug, and added a corn-flavored extract to his line. The other men were delighted that they had carried him on their backs while he was ailing, and paid him high compliments, but he thought they were making too much of his accomplishment. "I only did it because I wanted a drink more than anybody else," he has since diffidently explained.

By and large, the stragglers lived in harmony, but every now and then two of them would have a falling out. Whenever that happened, Yamamoto, whose comrades addressed him as "Commander," took pains to stay neutral. Had he sided with either disputant, the argument would have ended then and there, according to Japanese military custom. The loser in the squabble would also have lost considerable face, and that would have been awkward in such a small and close-knit community. To forestall such disputes, the Commander started making special efforts to keep his men cheerfully occupied. "It was important for me to sustain my men's morale, because I had one unwavering belief," he says. "After all that time, I didn't really expect the Japanese *Army* to come back for us, but I was convinced that the Japanese *people* couldn't be destroyed by a war, and I told my men that sooner or later *somebody* would be coming back for us. And when that happened—whenever it might be—I wanted at least one of us still to be alive, so he could report to the Japanese people that we had tried to do our best."

Yamamoto had graduated from a teachers' training school in 1942, and had taught school for a year before he became a soldier. Now, discovering that of his subordinates only one had finished high school and the majority had got nowhere near that far, he instituted regular academic sessions, during which his students sat around him in a circle, on logs. In this Mark Hopkins-like setting, he conducted classes, beginning with third-grade subjects. Nakano, whose protean talents included a flair for carpentry, made an abacus, which was a big help in elementary arithmetic. None of the pupils had any paper, so they scratched their lessons on slatelike stones. Yamamoto was gratified to observe that under his tutelage Izumida's writing, which had been atrocious, improved almost as rapidly as his banana cordial.

The Commander had a solitary pencil, and also a worn military map with a blank back. At the end of every day, he would jot diary notes on slats of wood, and once every couple of months he entered an abridgment of this bulky journal on the back of the map, in order to keep a permanent record. To buck up his own morale, he would periodically compose *haiku*, the lean, clipped verses so beloved by Japanese. "We know the purity of man only when exposed naked to each other," one of his poems went. To provide himself and his men with extracurricular diversion, he organized games. There were cerebral ones, like the traditional Go, and there were muscular ones, like leg-pushing and stone-throwing contests. The winners got an extra ration of pork or of hand-rolled cigarettes. In 1950, Yamamoto had his men build a little stage, and there they began to produce shows. The indefatigable Nakano manufactured bamboo flutes and other instruments. One of the most popular performances was a dramatization of Yamada's prize-winning love story about his sweetheart.

Sometimes, in the evenings, the stragglers would just sit around and talk. One night, they got onto the subject of an old Japanese legend, the tale of a young man named Urashima who had been kind to a turtle and as a result was invited to visit a magical palace beneath the sea. Life was so pleasant there that, in his blissful self-indulgence, he hardly gave a thought to his life at home, and when he returned to dry land after what had seemed to him a mere three years of submerged hedonism, he found that he was a white-haired old man. Yamamoto thought that the story pointed a moral for *his* men: that they must never, like Urashima, become so absorbed in their otherworldly existence on Mindoro as to stop thinking about their homeland, their families, and their own precious identities, all of which, some far-off day, might be theirs to reclaim.

Mindoro was, of course, no fairyland. However tolerable an existence the stragglers succeeded in wresting from the jungle, none of them was ever in really good health. The region abounded in fierce, insatiable leeches, and malaria was another dreadful, ever-present plague. Yamamoto became so despairingly feverish at one point that, in a spell of delirium, he resolved to blow himself up with a grenade, but one of his men snatched it away in time. The stragglers were constantly trying to decoct medicines. From a certain kind of grass they stewed a juice that seemed to relieve headaches and toothaches; the petals of a tiny rosebud, boiled in water, produced a syrup that they thought was good for stomach aches. Nevertheless, illness took a steady toll, and by June of 1951 five of the nine men had died.

The number four is considered unlucky in much of the Orient. It is associated with death, and, just as in the United States some office buildings pretend that they have no thirteenth story, Asian buildings ignore their fourth. Yet on Mindoro (as in Netherlands New Guinea) the number four proved to be lucky. After nearly twelve years of straggling, four Mindoro men were to come out alive. They were Yamamoto, Izumida, Nakano, and a soldier named Nitaro Ishii, who had been a miner in Akita Prefecture, in northwest Japan.

By mid-1951, Yamamoto, Izumida, Nakano, and Ishii had come to take it for granted that, unless illness or misadventure picked them off one by one, they would be together on their Mindoro hilltop for as long as they lived. But the more they talked about this interminable prospect, the more they began wondering about what was happening beyond Mount Ayamitan. There seemed to be only one reasonably safe way of making contact with the rest of the world, and that was through the Buhid. Curiosity finally impelled the Japanese to seek a reunion with the natives, and in the fall of 1954, after almost nine years of isolation, the stragglers once more ventured toward the neighboring village. This time, they brought with them a likely icebreaker—a batch of Izumida's finest banana brew. The Buhid had never before tasted liquor, and found it enchanting. In return, they gave the Japanese some salt—the first they'd had in nine years. The stragglers' systems were so unaccustomed to pure sodium chloride that when they first ate some of it their faces swelled up.

From then on, the Japanese and the natives fraternized continuously. (Rumors of this association reached an American anthropologist studying a native tribe a day's march from Yamamoto's settlement, but he was so busy recording indigenous mating songs that he didn't bother to seek out the Japanese. He later regeretted this; it would have been anthropologically rewarding to observe how two sets of persons with such different cultural backgrounds were getting along in the same natural environment.) The Buhid were not the most congenial or informative acquaintances imaginable. They were wholly unconcerned about what was going on across the next mountain, let alone in Manila or Tokyo. They were dirty, slovenly, superstitious, and, by Japanese standards, abysmally ignorant. They didn't even know their own ages; it was their custom to plant a tree when a baby was born, so whenever a straggler asked a native how old he was, the fellow would respond by pointing to a tree. Furthermore, Yamamoto had the impression that the natives indulged freely in incest. After he had learned enough of their language to be able to scold them, he reproached them for this. Calling their attention to a number of youngsters who, though their natal trees were straight and sturdy, were themselves pitiably misshapen, he informed them that incest was responsible for the deformities. The natives replied that this was nonsense; the unfortunate children had had a curse put on them by the spirits of cats and snails their elders had eaten. Yamamoto's possibly erroneous ideas about the prevalence of incest may have stemmed from the fact that in some Mangyan circles women habitually address all older men—including older husbands—as "Grandfather."

Most Mangyans being egalitarian, this village had no single chief, but there was one grandfather who was universally respected. Every so often, Yamamoto learned, a few of the natives would bestir themselves enough to walk to a village nearer the coast, and it occurred to him that if one of his men could go along, it might be possible to learn something of interest. The patriarch, however, said it was unthinkable for anyone to join such a sortie who did not belong to the tribe. To that Yamamoto had a ready reply: the old man had a marriageable daughter, and whoever became her husband would be a perfectly authentic member of the tribe, so why not give her hand to one of the stragglers? The old man thought this a logical enough proposition, but he said that Yamamoto was too tall for his girl, who, like many of her kinsmen, stood well under five feet. With Yamamoto eliminated because of size, and Izumida because he was already married, Ishii and Nakano were left. Ishii was the shorter of the two— about five feet three inches—and Yamamoto and the Buhid elder agreed that he would make a splendid bridegroom. Ishii had some reservations, but, coming from a land where arranged marriages are routine, and having been instructed by his superior officer to marry the girl, he put up only token resistance. (The bride, naturally, was not consulted.) The wedding date was set for early November, 1956.

This marriage of convenience never came off, for in October the four stragglers were returned to civilization. Ishii was quite relieved, but the Buhid were crushed. By that time, they had developed a powerful thirst, and were forever coming around to the stragglers' hut to cadge drinks. Unfortunately, they had never inquired how to make the stuff themselves, and now all at once their only source of supply had dried up. Izumida suspects that today those particular natives may be praying soberly to the god of their mountain for another war to be visited upon their parched terrain.

The news that there were Japanese living up among the hill people reached the coastal residents of Mindoro by way of a mineral prospector, who had heard about Yamamoto in the course of a trek into the interior in May, 1956. The trek lasted for four months, so it wasn't until late September, when the prospector arrived at the east-coast port of Roxas, that he was able to inform anybody of his discovery. He said that the inland natives who had told him about the Japanese had called their commander "Tonari." This information was correct. The four stragglers had decided some time earlier that they would conceal their identities from the Mangyans by using nicknames. For all they knew, they were being sought, under their real names, as war criminals. Accordingly, Yamamoto became "Tonari," which in Japanese means "neighbor;" Ishii, who had served briefly on Cebu Island, became "Cebuto;" Izumida, who was then in his early forties, and nearly a decade older than the others, became "Jiisan," a variant of the Japanese for "grandpa;" and Nakano became "Taro," a common Japanese first name.

Formal diplomatic relations between Japan and the Philippines had been resumed only in July of 1956, and when the newly posted Japanese ambassador in Manila, Koichiro Asakai (subsequently his country's envoy in Washington), heard the report from Roxas, he asked the Philippine government to pluck the stragglers from their mountain hideaway and deliver them, intact, into Japanese hands. The rescue job was entrusted to the Philippine Constabulary, a national military-police force that was established under United States auspices in 1901 and, because of the colorful shoulder tabs on its uniforms, is known as the Khaki and the Red. General Manuel Cabal, who was then head of the Constabulary (he was later chief of staff of his nation's Army), held a conference in Manila, which the mayor of Roxas, a small-town politician named Francisco Pamero, was invited to attend. Pamero informed his fellow-conferees—none of whom had any reason not to believe him—that he had actually been to the stragglers' lair, that the place was a four-day march from Roxas, and that there were fifty-three Japanese in the group, led by an English-speaking captain named Murai. Pamero added that some of the soldiers lived in caves and some in treetops, and that at least three had married Mangyans and raised families. Cabal ordered the Constabulary to mount an expedition, of which friendliness was to be the keynote. Its members were equipped with gifts for the stragglers—whiskey, *sake*, cigarettes, rice—and also with placatory gifts, mostly of the bead and trinket variety, for the Mangyans, who, it was rumored, might be inclined to shower poisoned arrows upon trespassers. The very name of the task force was a pun brimming with amiability. The Japanese word for "friend" is *"tomodachi,"* which, in parts of Asia, where transliteration is far from an exact science, has become *"tumadachi."* The expedition, which would be operating in the Second Military Area of the Philippines, was accordingly called "Task Force IIMADachi" (the last two syllables here having no independent meaning, but being thrown in just to go along with the gag), pronounced "Tumadachi."

The original plan was for Mayor Pamero to return to the stragglers' home and negotiate with them; he would carry a powerful radio, over which, if the Japanese proved amenable, he could send back word for the Constabulary to come on in. The Japanese soldiers, Cabal and his aides reasoned, would be more hospitable, or at any rate less hostile, to a civilian than to a military courier. In case Pamero couldn't make it all the way to the Japanese camp this time, General Cabal had some bilingual safe-conduct passes printed up, to be air-dropped to the stragglers. These instructed the recipients, in Japanese, to march to a clearing, carrying a bamboo stick with a piece of cloth or paper, or even some leaves, attached; to carry their weapons, if any, at the position of sling arms, unloaded, with the barrels pointing down; and, when they reached the clearing, to pile up their weapons in one place and their ammunition in another, and wait there until they heard from the Constabulary. In English, the safe-conduct passes read, "The Japanese soldier who carries this safe-conduct pass is using it as a sign of his sincere wish to come down and live in peace. He should be given full protection, food, and medical attention by members of the armed forces of the Philippines." At the same time, Toyokichi Nakagawa, the First Secretary of the Japanese Embassy in Manila, prepared a long letter to the *zanryūsha*, which went, in part:

We are trying to get you back. We have heard from the Filipinos and the Constabulary that there are fifty of you on Mindoro. Japan surrendered eleven years ago. Now we are rebuilding Japan fast. You'll see no traces of war—just prosperity. Your families and the Japanese people are looking forward to your return. On July 23, 1956, Japan and the Philippines established formal diplomatic relations, and ambassadors were exchanged. . . . Cultural exchanges are frequent now between the two countries. More than one hundred Japanese businessmen are living in Manila. Many Japanese ships put into Philippine ports, to load up with iron and timber. . . . The primary thing we want you to know is that the Japanese-Filipino war is over, and that you're going to come back not as prisoners but as fine, upstanding Japanese. We can't help admiring the patience and self-control you've displayed in your eleven years of suffering. Next, we want to tell you that the Japanese Embassy in the Philippines has guarantees from the Philippine government about your safety. So long as you don't shoot, there will be no shooting from the Philippine side. . . . Those of you who have married natives have the choice of bringing your families back

or coming out alone. . . . Looking forward to the day
when we will see you . . .

Task Force Tumadachi was scheduled to get moving on October 22nd, and on that day its leader learned
from an apologetic Mayor Pamero that he had never laid
eyes on any of the Japanese and had imagined all his de-
tails about them. Pamero was still given a place in the
advance party, however—now not because of superior
knowledge but because he wanted to atone for his previous mistake. The party, with a former guerrilla fighter
from northern Mindoro named Lucio Daguno in charge,
consisted of twenty-eight men—civilians, soldiers, signal-
men, medical-aid men, bearers, Mayor Pamero, and two
Mangyan interpreters—none of them in uniform. On the
afternoon of October 24, 1956, as they climbed the stragglers' mountain, the Mangyan interpreters ran into Ishii,
who was out for a stroll, clad in a G string. As they approached him, they cried out "Tumadachi!" and ostenta-
tiously pointed their weapons toward the ground. Ishii
was wary, but he let them come close enough to hand
over the First Secretary's letter. Then he told them to
stay where they were, and rushed back to the stragglers'
hut, waving the letter excitedly. Yamamoto took it, read
it to himself, and then read it aloud. What, he asked, did
the others make of it? None of them could quite believe
what it said, but none of them were willing to ignore it.
Finally, it was agreed that Yamamoto should go and talk
to the Filipinos. If he didn't return in a reasonable time,
the others would assume that he'd met with foul play,
and would commit suicide.

Yamamoto put on his officer's tunic—rather, the tattered remnants of it—and marched to the rendezvous. When he met the waiting men, one of them addressed him in Japanese, and Yamamoto asked, "Are Filipinos and Japanese friends now?"

"Yes," said the Filipino.

"If we come down, will the lowlanders hurt us?" Yamamota asked.

"If they do, we will shoot them."

"Very good," said Yamamoto.

He invited the rescue party to accompany him to the stragglers' hut. That night, the four Japanese, dazed by the good fortune that appeared to have befallen them, treated their guests, themselves dazed by the comparative elegance of the stragglers' home life, to a feast of roast chicken and roast pork. After dinner, one of Izumida's jugs was fraternally passed around, and soon all voices were joined in convivial harmony. A medical-aid man gave the Japanese some vitamin shots, and also dosed them with assorted pills and tonics. Yet not even all this cozy camaraderie induced the Japanese to unbend completely. Three days were to pass before they divulged their real names.

The Constabulary had hoped to evacuate the stragglers by helicopter, but after Daguno's men had spent three days clearing a landing area on a slope of Mount Ayamitan, the pilot of their copter declined to risk alighting on such uneven terrain. The stragglers therefore had to walk to a lower-level clearing, whence they were transported, by several stages, to the Khaki and the Red headquarters, in Quezon City, just outside Manila. For their

arrival, all four men were decked out in new uniforms—
that is to say, in clean sets of the long since outmoded
trappings of the no longer existing Imperial Army—presumably obtained from some almost forgotten stockpile
of Japanese Army surplus in the Philippines. The men
were feeble, and they were sick, and they were thin, but
upon catching sight of a welcoming committee, they
snapped to attention and marched toward it with military precision. Then, standing stiffly in formation, they
produced their homemade musical instruments and
briskly rendered the Japanese national anthem.

A few weeks later, the four men were home. Aboard the
ship that took them to Japan, Yamamoto conscientiously
wrote a report to his government on their experiences.
In this, he revealed how concerned he and his companions were about a dismaying turn of events they'd learned
of. Izumida's wife and sons, it developed, had been notified in 1944 that he was dead, whereupon his wife had
married Izumida's younger brother, by whom she had
since had three more children. Reflecting on this do-
mestic snarl, Yamamoto wrote, "I suppose if you can go
back in history and live a primitive jungle existence, you
can also go forward again and solve your personal problems in modern civilization." But the problem was, of
course, Izumida's. He decided that he would gallantly
leave the status quo undisturbed. "I planned to go off
somewhere else and not be a bother to anyone," he recalled recently. "But my father was dead, and my uncles
said that as the eldest son in my family I should take
charge of it again, and remarry my wife. So I did. My

brother left, with his three children, and married someone else. My wife was upset when I first got home, but
everything has worked out fine, and now, with our sons
off at school, we're tending our farm together, just the
two of us." The reunited Izumidas grow rice and tange-
rines on a two-and-a-half-acre farm three miles outside
the resurrected city of Nagasaki. Izumida has pretty well
settled back into the humdrum routine of a Japanese
farmer, but his neighbors still josh him every so often
about his peculiar history; whenever he does something
that strikes them as unconventional, they like to say,
"Oh, you must be doing it the Mindoro way."

Nakano and Ishii have both married since their repatriation, and both have children. Nakano has gone
back to barbering. Ishii—who after his wedding adopted
his wife's surname, Sato—is now employed as a lumber
salesman. Yamamoto, back in Wakayama Prefecture, is
teaching mathematics to a ninth-grade class at Tanabe,
and is also serving as its vocational-guidance counsellor.
Known as the Mindoro Teacher, he has become something of a campus celebrity. Most of his students are fifteen or sixteen, so this year's flock was born after he
began conducting classes on Mindoro. He feels that he
has a peculiarly strong obligation to impress upon his pupils the horrors of warfare and to instill in them a
dedication to pursue peaceful vocations. Yamamoto was
the last of his group to get married, having held back
out of fear that a dozen years of celibacy might have per-
manently undermined his virility. Then he overcame his
apprehensions and married a local girl. They have one
daughter, on whom he dotes. "Being with my family

makes me feel new again," he says. By now, he is so far from being disturbed about any loss of manhood that he can share in sexual jests about his strange past. In October, 1960, his school held a carnival, one feature of which was a beauty contest. The students in his class gigglingly dressed him up in a grass skirt, a white brassière, outsize earrings, and their version of a Mangyan belle's headdress. Then, while his friends and neighbors joined in the applause, the children fondly paraded him around the school athletic field behind a placard identifying him as "Miss Mindoro."

6

COME
BACK,
HIRO-CHAN!

Most of the *zanryūsha* had no idea, as they huddled incommunicado in their island hideouts, that there were other Japanese in similar predicaments. Upon arriving home, Yamamoto was amazed to learn of the widespread and enigmatic notoriety that had been achieved by Hiroo Onoda, the lieutenant he'd flown with to the Philippines twelve years earlier. Onoda was one of the very few stragglers who were known to be at large, or to have been at large, on a particular island. The first word about him was received on July 5, 1950, in the coastal village of Looc, in southeast Lubang. Early one morning, some of Looc's residents were approached by a supplicant Japanese, gaunt and half naked, his belly swollen from malnutrition. The natives ran away from him, but he plodded after them, and when they finally decided he meant them no ill, they let him come close. He was so filthy that the Looc villagers, whose own standards of personal daintiness were not lofty, at once handed him a cake of soap and directed him to the sea, where, working up the best lather he could, he scrubbed himself while the townsfolk looked on. As soon as he was presentable, he was brought face to face with a Filipino who understood Japanese, and began to tell his story. It was a typical war-end narrative of defeat, disintegration, and despair.

This straggler, Yuichi Akatsu, an Army private, was also one of a quartet of survivors from a much larger group. He had not seen the three others—Private Kinshichi Kosuka, Sergeant Shoichi Shimada, and Lieutenant Onoda—since an after-dark food-gathering excursion eight months before, in the course of which he'd become separated from them, but at that time all three had been in fairly sound shape. The life of the stragglers on Lubang, it developed as Akatsu's tale unfolded, was quite different from that of the Japanese on Mindoro. Lubang is a small island; one can walk across it in half a day. The island consists of hilly jungle ringed by beach sands of exceptional whiteness. (One of Lubang's few commercial products is sand; because of its purity, the Philippines' largest brewers, the firm of San Miguel, fancy it for bottle glass.) Most of the ten thousand inhabitants of Lubang are littoral, but they get up into the hills often enough so that it would be difficult to clear and cultivate a tract of land without being detected. These four Japanese, accordingly, had never dared try to do what Yamamoto's crew was doing. Instead, they had lived like hunted animals, moving from one den to another and grabbing whatever sustenance—bananas, coconuts, an occasional stray carabao—they came across. They were all that was left, as far as they knew, of a garrison of two hundred and fifty that had been smashed when United States forces retook Lubang, in March, 1945. That fall, the Allies had showered leaflets upon the little island, reporting the end

of the war and admonishing the seventy-odd Japanese
then believed to be there to surrender. Onoda, the only
officer among them, had previously been told by his superiors that the war in the Philippines might very well
go on for twenty or thirty years, so he was not to be
swayed by any such enemy blandishments. In February,
1946, the Americans tracked down and killed several of
the remaining Japanese and, by means of persuasive
broadcasts over portable loudspeakers, cajoled some forty
others into giving up. Onoda still did not believe that the
war had ended, but Akatsu was less certain. "Somebody
found a Japanese newspaper that a search party had put
out for us," Akatsu said recently. "Reading it, I thought
that the war might possibly be over. I thought so again
in 1948, when I saw a light in a lighthouse that up to
then had been blacked out. Maybe the others had
thoughts like mine, but if so, we didn't talk about them.
And we could never be *sure*. One surrender leaflet I saw
was written in incorrect Japanese (this was the one with
the suspect *"kōfuku"* in it), and I was certain that leaflet was a Yankee trick. In any case, however we may have
felt inwardly, we all pretended to be skeptical of any evidence we saw or heard, and we bragged how we were
going to remain soldiers for as long as necessary."

The four intractable unbelievers had little in common. Akatsu is a short, shy, frail, soft-spoken man whose
family has long scratched out a living by making children's hats in their Tokyo home. Being a city boy, he had
had a difficult time keeping up with the others on Lubang
when they went out foraging, for the pace was usually set
by Sergeant Shimada, a tough, muscular man from

mountain country. Kosuka, like Akatsu, was a mere private, but he felt nowhere near as subservient as Akatsu did to the sergeant and the lieutenant. A slick, self-assured fellow who had once been a jockey, Kosuka was, if not a professional gambler, an accomplished amateur. Also, in his home town of Hachioji, outside Tokyo, he had often been called upon to serve as a master of ceremonies at local fêtes; just about the only entertainment the four men had on Lubang was provided by Kosuka, who at night would mount an imaginary stage and give recitations, or would pick up a nonexistent telephone and make gossipy long-distance calls to his sporting cronies back home. Hiroo Onoda, one of six children of an executive of an insecticide firm, had been raised in relatively well-to-do circumstances. An elder brother, Toshio, was a doctor. Hiroo—known to his family as Hiro-chan, Kanro, or Kan—had finished high school, where he had been proficient at *kendo*, a Japanese form of fencing. He had fought in China for a year and a half as an enlisted man, and had then been tapped for training as an officer.

The lieutenant was a courageous and dedicated soldier, but he was young—only twenty-four in 1945—and somewhat irresolute. He often conferred with and deferred to Sergeant Shimada, who was seven years his senior. In the spring of 1946, when the United States was making another diligent effort to persuade the Japanese on Lubang to come out of hiding, Onoda wavered briefly. The four holdouts came upon a letter written by one of the forty Japanese who had surrendered, which called upon them to follow their comrades' example, and which had a map attached showing where they should go.

COME BACK, HIRO-CHAN!

Onoda said that, as leader of the group, he owed it to his men at least to investigate this proposal. He would go to the designated rendezvous alone, he told them, and signal the others with revolver shots, telling them either to follow him or to flee. Shimada, however, began to raise objections. "In ordinary circumstances," Akatsu has since explained, "everybody has to obey his commander, but the sergeant was a bigger man than the lieutenant, and much more forceful. I had been listening to them discuss the matter, and when the lieutenant said he'd go off alone, even if it meant being shot or imprisoned, I was glad to hear such brave talk from my commanding officer. I was sorry I couldn't speak up, but, of course, being a private, I could only listen. Kosuka was different. Private or not, he always spoke his mind, and he always sided with Shimada. So the two of them persuaded the lieutenant not to make a move. Oh, I was shaken and saddened! Six months later, Lieutenant Onoda got to talking to me confidentially one day, while Shimada and Kosuka were somewhere else, and he told me that he was afraid we'd lost our last chance to leave Lubang alive. 'Oh, what I wouldn't give for one more chance like that!' he said."

Akatsu proved to have been a good listener. Early in 1951, after spending six months in Quezon City recuperating from his ordeal on Lubang, he returned to Japan, where he met the families of his three fellow-stragglers and staggered them with his intimate knowledge of their home lives. He himself soon went back to making children's hats, and he is still making them today, in a

cramped house in the Daito-ku section of Tokyo, in col-
laboration with his wife (he got married in 1957), his
father, his mother, a sister, and two brothers and their
wives. By now, too, he has a boy and a girl of his own to
make hats for. "I don't blame anybody for what happened to me on Lubang," Akatsu says. "I just had a spell
of bad luck, and, compared to many Japanese soldiers,
I guess I had some good luck, too, because when I got
home I found all of my family living and not in any trouble, and I could pick up my life where I'd left it."

The relatives of Akatsu's comrades on Lubang were
understandably hopeful that some good fortune would
come their soldiers' way as well, and they began implor-
ing their government to do something about rounding up
Onoda, Shimada, and Kosuka. It was Akatsu's belief that
the three men would surrender peaceably only if they
were summoned forth by other Japanese—preferably by
Japanese known to them. But there were complications.
In 1951, relations between the Philippines and Japan
were still icy, and in Manila there was little enthusiasm
for letting any Japanese, however merciful their mission,
set foot on the soil that their countrymen had so lately
bloodied. Besides, said the Philippine authorities, they
couldn't insure the safety of any wandering Japanese, in
view of the deep resentment that the Filipino people still
felt toward their wartime tormentors.

One of the first Japanese who *were* allowed to enter
the Philippines in the postwar years got to Manila in
February, 1952. He was a former lieutenant colonel
named Nobuhiko Jimbo, who had been instrumental in
saving the wartime president of the Philippines, the late

Manuel Roxas, from execution at Japanese hands. Roxas had subsequently interceded when, after V-J Day, Jimbo was about to be executed by the Chinese Nationalists for war crimes he had allegedly committed during a tour of duty in China. Now, having entered the export-import business, and having come to Manila to try to stimulate the flow of bananas between the Philippines and Japan, Jimbo heard about the Lubang stragglers. Being a man with a flair for publicizing himself, he offered to fly over that island and lure them forth. General Cabal, of the Constabulary, lent him a light plane equipped with a loudspeaker, and Jimbo made a few low-level passes over Lubang, shouting, among other things, "I am Jimbo!" and, after that thunderous salutation, urging his auditors to walk to the nearest village and turn themselves in. Nothing happened, conceivably because the name Jimbo meant nothing to anyone beneath the Colonel's flight path. Shortly after landing, he declared that there were a thousand Japanese soldiers still at large in the Philippines, but he has never divulged how he hit upon that figure.

During the next couple of years, the Japanese would periodically ask the Philippine government to let them scour Lubang for Onoda and his companions, but they were consistently turned down until the spring of 1954. On May 7th of that year, a Constabulary unit routinely patrolling Lubang ran into three Japanese, and a gun-fight ensued. One Japanese was killed, but the others got away, leaving a trail of blood that petered out inconclusively. The victim was Shimada. Whether just one or both of the others, who were presumed to be Onoda and

Kosuka, had been wounded, and whether seriously, no one could tell. Perhaps one man or both had crawled into the bush and died. Perhaps one or both had been gravely enough hurt to commit suicide. Perhaps the loss of Shimada, on whose strength, according to Akatsu, the others had so heavily relied, would ultimately cause a companion to kill himself even if he was not seriously injured.

In any event, three days after that skirmish, Manila sent word to Tokyo that the Japanese could go to Lubang and have a look around for themselves. Before the end of May, Dr. Onoda, the lieutenant's older brother, who was serving as an internist at the Metropolitan Police Hospital in Tokyo, and Kosuka's younger brother Fukuji, who was a farmer at Hachioji, were in Manila, accompanied by a representative of their government's Ministry of Health and Welfare. The three men next chartered a light plane and, as Jimbo had done, flew over Lubang and announced their presence by means of a loudspeaker. Then they took a boat to Lubang, where they were restrained by the local authorities from exploring the depths of the jungle but allowed to spend two weeks poking around its edges. They found no trace of either quarry, and returned to Japan as unenlightened as when they'd left.

As time passed, new rumors about the two *zanryū-sha* were vigorously spawned and spread around Lubang. Both men had married native women and were raising families, it was said—though nobody had any first-hand, or even second-hand, evidence to substantiate the hypothesis. Another yarn had it that the stragglers were unwilling to come out because they had dug up a buried treasure—gold, millions of pesos' worth of gold—and were jealously hoarding it against God knew what eventuality. More ominously, news would regularly come out of Lubang of the killing or maiming of islanders by elusive assailants who were usually claimed, by the victims or other eyewitnesses, to have a strikingly Japanese appearance. In 1956 alone, stragglers were accused of murdering seven Lubang residents. Who could the dastardly criminals be, chorused the people of Lubang, but Onoda and Kosuka? (That there was some basis for such a surmise was conceded not long ago by Akatsu, who acknowledged that in the immediate post-war years, at least, Onoda and his roving band had done some shooting in deadly earnest. "I don't know how many Filipinos we killed on Lubang while I was there," Akatsu says, "but we killed some, and that is a fact.") The reports incriminating the Japanese were received with considerable skepticism by the Philippine Constabulary. What better way, the police reasoned, for an assassin on Lubang to escape punishment for his crimes than to blame them on elusive stragglers? Violence was not unknown on the island, yet now it seemed that no resident of that area ever took a pot shot at another; it was always those pesky Japanese. (In a novel entitled "The Isle of Lubang," published in Japan in 1958, the author also credited five stragglers on Lubang—a second lieutenant and four enlisted men— with rape and infanticide; no such charges have been levelled by anybody against these characters' real-life prototypes.)

The skepticism of the Constabulary was shared by

Colonel Itagaki's Repatriation Section in Tokyo. (That the men on Lubang were aware of its earnest efforts was shown by the discovery in Shimada's pocket of a worn handbill the Section had prepared.) But as Itagaki kept hearing about strange goings on in the hills of Lubang (and once even on the beach, where a bullet zipped past the ear of the Japanese consul from Manila, who was taking time off from a leaflet-strewing mission for a swim), he could not help feeling that sufficient uncertainty existed to warrant his making a further investigation. Accordingly, his Section began drawing up plans for a new, two-phase expedition, which would be, essentially, a larger-scale version of the 1954 venture. To begin with, the island would be bombed once monthly, for six months, with ten thousand leaflets, plus some Japanese newspapers, magazines, books, and candy. It was hoped that if the two fugitives were alive, they would respond to all this by leaving a message at a junction of more or less well-travelled trails. Then a Japanese search party would go to the scene and meet them.

On the afternoon of January 27, 1959, fourteen years after Lieutenant Onoda had landed on Lubang, some civilians cutting logs outside the coastal village of Calingag were fired on. One man was wounded, and two carabao nearby were killed. A Constabulary soldier presently arrived on the scene, and was told that the aggressors were Japanese stragglers. "Well built and stocky, with long hair" was the description that he received, and he passed it along by radio to his superiors on Mindoro. As soon as word of this latest outrage on Lubang had been relayed up the Khaki and the Red chain of command, questions were sent back. Mindoro was asked:

> PCZBX 0129 dash 146 pd Reurad MAB 0129-19 cma ans folwg EEIs cln how many more Jap stragglers are in Lubang Is query what part of Lubang Is are they hiding query what are their arms query how do they subsist query do they have contact with civilians query if so cma who are their contacts query were there empty shells recovered in the crime scene query were there [sic] civilians who actually saw the Jap stragglers before and after the incident pd Flash ans imdtly.

It took Mindoro two days to flash its answer, which, aside from a suggestion that the assailants might have been after the carabao, and might have been unaware at first that there were men in the vicinity, was not illuminating. The only subsequent item of interest was that although no cartridge cases could be found near the scene of the shooting, the slugs removed from the brains of the dead carabao, which were sent out for laboratory examination, proved to be not of Japanese origin.

Just a week after the Calingag shooting, a laborer in Ambulong, some five miles away, was fatally shot by two men who were once again positively identified by onlookers as Japanese stragglers. The Constabulary, which by this time was under the command of another veteran Army officer, General Isagani V. Campo, decided to accelerate its on-and-off pursuit of these will-o'-the-wisps. Campo, a suave, shrewd, hard-boiled man, who even when out of uniform carries a heavy gold-plated, knob-studded metal club, gave orders that the ten-man Constabulary detachment on Lubang should be reinforced and also that some dogs trained for man hunts should be dispatched to the island. Still, Campo was determined to temper his justice with mercy. On February 5th, two days after the Ambulong assault, he sent a message addressed "To the People of Lubang." It read:

> For your own safety, please notify immediately the Philippine Constabulary or any member of the police force as to the whereabouts of or where you have last seen the Japanese soldiers who, up to now, are still in the vicinity of Lubang Island. I am appealing to you, as much as possible, not to harm them and let the peace officers deal with them. Thank you very much.

Notwithstanding Campo's temperate instructions, the reaction in Japan to this new move was that the Constabulary was out to bag Onoda and Kosuka on a dead-or-alive basis, and word got around that the peace officers, far from wishing not to harm the two men, would probably shoot them down like dogs—if, indeed, the peace officers' dogs did not chew them up first. The people of Japan were aroused. Kosuka's elderly parents made a pilgrimage from their farm to the Philippine Embassy in Tokyo to plead that their son's life be spared. The Japanese Diet became agitated; its Liberal-Democrat and Socialist members, who rarely agree about anything, announced that they were unanimously resolved to act—though they were not quite sure what action they should or could take. In the best parliamentary tradition, the Repatriation Committee of the House of Representatives proceeded to hold hearings. Yuichi

COME BACK, HIRO-CHAN!

Akatsu stopped making children's hats long enough to
testify, and reiterated his conviction that his erstwhile
companions would never surrender unless they were
sought out by close friends or relatives. Chasing them
would never work, he asserted; someone would have to go
into the jungle and wait there for the stragglers to make
the first conciliatory gesture. He said he was willing to go
back to Lubang himself if it would help any. Lieutenant
Onoda's mother, aged seventy-three, declared that *she*
would go to Lubang, where, she said, she would willingly
trade her life for her Hiro-chan's. It became known that
every single night since he'd been reported missing she
had dreamed about him, and every day, at every meal,
she had set a place for him at the family table; she would
put food at his place, stare mournfully at his untouched
plate, and burst into tears. A Lions Club in Osaka offered
to pay her way to Lubang, and the club appealed to
President Carlos Garcia of the Philippines, a Lion himself, to stay his people's itchy trigger fingers.

All over Japan, a Spare the Stragglers campaign got
rolling. In Tokyo, a visiting Manila clergyman, who had
survived the Bataan Death March, volunteered to carry
back to his homeland a recorded message from Mrs.
Onoda to her son. A Tokyo Rotary Club asked Rotary in
Manila to intercede, and appended to its request a fifty-
dollar solatium for the family of the last Lubang man
whom the stragglers were thought to have murdered. The
Japanese Disabled Veterans Association appealed to the
United Disabled Veterans Association of the Philippines,
and the Boy Scouts in Tokyo to their opposite numbers
in Manila. Three hundred thousand Japanese signed

petitions to the Philippine government asking that Onoda and Kosuka be given a break. Mrs. Onoda, escorted by eight schoolmates of her missing son and assisted by Akatsu, distributed ten thousand handbills at Tokyo's main railroad station. Office workers strolling by sobbed at the sight of the distraught mother, and one stenographer impetuously offered to do her bit by marrying either man. (She somewhat marred the beauty of this gesture by adding that she imagined she and her husband could live nicely off the proceeds from his account of his adventure.) The Japanese government was told by one helpful citizen that the surest way of luring the stragglers out of hiding would be by sending attractive young Japanese women into the jungle, as live bait. Another unsolicited bit of advice was that a platoon of men costumed in Imperial Army uniforms should be sent to the wilds of Lubang and should establish a camp there. Sooner or later, as the man who conceived this scheme predicted, the nostalgic enclave would prove an irresistible magnet.

Late in February, the Diet gave its blessing to the Repatriation Section's search plans, and allocated eight million yen—about twenty-two thousand dollars—to implement them. This was the only time in the whole postwar era that Japan earmarked a specific sum to rescue specific men in a specific area, and it was ironic that this unparalleled effort should have been made on behalf of two men who had very possibly died some five years earlier. The Philippine government voiced no objections to the Japanese endeavor. Then, in mid-March, before the sluggish wheels of bureaucracy could start turning,

two more Lubang natives were reported to have been
shot at, but in this instance not hit, by stragglers—although, to be sure, both this information and the inform-
ant who submitted it were evaluated by the Constabulary
as extremely unreliable.

Itagaki and his associates at the Repatriation Section
recruited several volunteers to aid them. It had been decided by now that Mrs. Onoda was simply too old and
infirm to go slogging around in a jungle, but her doctor
son, Toshio, offered once more to go to Lubang, and so
did Kosuka's brother Fukuji, and so, again, did Akatsu.
Another ex-soldier, Yoshio Fujita, a telephone-company
technician who had served on the island with the missing
men, also volunteered to go along. It was felt, though,
that before any of them went to Lubang, the two stragglers, who by this time were presumably adamant in their
determination not to be captured alive, would have to be
softened up. To that end, Itagaki planned to subject
them to an almost incessant two-month bombardment
of electronically amplified appeals—from loudspeakers
on Lubang, on ships cruising along its shoreline, and on
planes flying overhead. A well-known ballad singer in
Japan, Yoshio Tabata, recorded a few tunes that it was
hoped would melt the stragglers' frosty indifference—
among them "A Night in China," "Cry for Love," and
"A Little Coffee Shop." Other popular vocalists recorded
children's songs ("The Ball," "The Road," "The Ca-
nary," and "Shoes Are Singing"), martial songs (the
anthem "Kimigayo," "Battleship March," and "War
Friends"), and *bushi,* which are folk songs often rendered
in geisha houses.

To gather material for the principal broadcasts, tape recorders were set up in Onoda's and Kosuka's homes, and their relatives began to talk away ad lib. All of them, beginning with Kosuka's father, who urged him to come home and get married, tried to jog the fugitives' conceivably dim memories and to persuade them that what they were hearing was true.

Kosuka's mother reminisced:

> I remember clearly how as a child you didn't like to wear clothes or shoes, and liked worms and bugs. . . . Do you remember that you got your first job in the village office? You were going to take a census, but you didn't do a good job of it. You remember *that*, don't you?

His brother Fukuji said:

> You and I used to ride horses together. You remember my voice, don't you? I'm a man now, helping our father. All your friends are grown up and have children. Come on back. Everything has changed in the city where I'm staying. We have two nice new school buildings. Your sister's children have grown up and graduated from junior high school. Come back and join us horse-back-riding. Your father and mother are old. We need you. Come back soon. You know my voice. Believe me.

A younger sister said:

> I remember seeing you off at the station, with many Japanese flags. You looked so happy when you joined the Army. At that time it was only natural; everybody wanted to be a soldier for his country. If you're still thinking that way now, it would be ironic. When I see other

COME BACK, HIRO-CHAN!

men your age, it makes me sad to think that you're living in the jungle. We talked to Akatsu. I can't understand why *you* don't come back, too. The mountains are green. You'd be surprised to see me, so big and grown up. I'm working at the bank, counting money all day long. I really want to see you again.

And an elder sister:

Your cousin was only two when you left; now he's in high school. When you were young, you were stung by bees up on the mountain. Remember? You were lying on the ground, and your friends ran back for help, and your father went to the mountain and brought you home. You were crying with pain. Remember that? Every morning, when you got up, you would first rub down your horse. Remember that? Remember all these things, and come back home. . . .

Then she sang a *shingunka*, a song often sung in past years to cheer up soldiers, or sung on the march by soldiers to cheer themselves up.

Lieutenant Onoda's father, after a good deal of choked-up throat-clearing, told his son that relations between Japan and the Philippines were pleasant, and begged him to read and heed the literature that he could not miss finding somewhere on Lubang. Onoda's mother tried to sing her son a *shingunka*, too, but it came out all sniffles. Then she reminded him that he had once been entered in a baby contest:

You got first prize. You don't remember that, of course, but we have the pictures. . . . When your grandfather died, you went to the funeral. When you were

in the third grade of primary school, you went swim-
ming, and you told me how far you swam. You said you
swam ten thousand metres. You remember *that*, don't
you?

Lieutenant Yamamoto had returned home after a long
self-imposed exile on Mindoro, she informed him, and
added:

When your friend came back from Mindoro, he felt
so at home with *his* mother. So why don't you come out
and join me? *Please* come out.

One of Onoda's sisters dwelt on how he and she
had often scuffled playfully as children:

If you want to fight somebody, why don't you come
back and fight with me? Japan has changed so much.
It's at peace. There are many things awaiting you that
you can't imagine. Your mother went to Tokyo and
talked to the Diet. Your mother and father are at home
now. Why don't you come back and let them see you
before they die? Come back, Hiro-chan!

Equipped with some of postwar Japan's most re-
splendent electronic devices, including one bulky ampli-
fier that, suspended from two poles, required fourteen
bearers to transport it overland, the first wave of the
Japanese search party hit the white beaches of Lubang
early in May, 1959. In charge was Itagaki's deputy, Yuzo
Miura, a kindly, lanky, prognathous man, who had spent
several weeks conferring with psychologists, hoping
thereby, like a novice angler consulting a savvy Indian
guide, to glean some tips on the best lures for a mad-

deningly elusive species of fish. Miura and a couple of
aides took with them sixty tons of presumably enticing
impedimenta, including twenty dozen bottles of Japanese beer and such choice edibles as *yokan,* a candy
made of red beans, and dried seaweed. They also carried
three large paper kites in the shape of carp, which Japanese boys habitually fly on their third, fifth, and seventh
birthdays, and the sight of which, Miura's psychologists
thought, ought to make any grown-up Japanese boy who
had not taken utter leave of his senses irrepressibly homesick.

The quest got off to a dismal start. While the
rescuers were cruising off Lubang, broadcasting from a
boat that flew a large Japanese flag at the top of its
mast, Fujita, the telephone-company man, fell overboard
and hurt himself. Then, almost as soon as the party
landed on the island, one of its members bumped into a
nest of bees. Miura, who was directly in the path of the
swarm, fell to the ground, stung a thousand times, and
had to be taken by litter to the nearest hospital. It was
small comfort to him to learn, on being released a week
later, that he and his men had flushed a kind of bee
not theretofore known to have inhabited Lubang. It was
smaller comfort when the Manila *Chronicle,* in a waspish
editorial a few days later, described his expedition as
"rather Quixotic" and, after expressing its belief that the
bees were just about the only living creatures that any
Japanese were ever likely to discover on Lubang, said
that it was high time the Philippine Constabulary got
down to business and began stalking the stragglers as

common criminals, "not as a couple of visionaries who shun living in a world under a temporary truce."

Disregarding such strictures, Miura's party went about its business, which included placing at various spots on the island—a river bank, the intersection of two streams, the crossing of two trails, a conspicuous rock in a coconut grove, the entrance to a cave, and so on— ten white wooden mailboxes, prominently identified by Japanese flags and inscriptions, and containing writing paper, pencils, envelopes, and copies of letters written to Onoda and Kosuka by their parents. To help the stragglers find these receptacles, each of which was to be opened by the searchers every two weeks, the Japanese Embassy in Manila printed maps showing their sites, and these were dropped from the air, along with thousands of pieces of beckoning literature. The missing men were urged to respond to the broadcasts in any way they chose—by written word, by shouting, by hand signals, by waving a cloth, by anything. But please, by *something*. The mailboxes were scrupulously checked every second week. Aside from the fact that birds had nested on one of them, they seemed untouched. On the ground near another one, Miura's party did find a torn-off khaki-colored trouser leg. However, the trouser leg, unlike those on wartime Japanese uniforms, was cuffed, and, further-more, a laboratory examination disclosed that it was made in part of nylon fibres, which were not used by the Japanese textile industry until 1951. With nothing more to show for his dogged efforts than this hunk of cloth and a paper packet full of bee stingers that had been extracted

from his throbbing body, Miura retreated to Japan with
his team.

After a lull during the summer rainy season, Miura's
boss, Itagaki, arrived on Lubang and swung into action,
accompanied by eighty Filipinos—Lubang natives, Constabulary soldiers, and Army engineers. (He brought
along another load of persuasive material, such as copies
of a special edition the weekly *Asahi Graphic* had put
out in tribute to the Crown Prince's marrying a com-
moner. Surely any Japanese who saw this spread, it was
reasoned, would deduce that a new and peaceful state
of affairs prevailed in his homeland.) Akatsu was there,
too, and scarcely had he set foot on the island that had
treated him so harshly for so long when he was prostrated
by a raging fever. But after a week he was back on his
feet, enjoying the novel pleasure of being able to walk
around Lubang in broad daylight without any need to
fret about what might be lurking behind each tree. The
missing men's brothers had come back, too, and their
arrival had been heralded by the dissemination of still
more leaflets. One addressed to Kosuka read, in part:

> Hey, brother! It's me—your kid brother, Fukuji. . . .
> Don't you want to come home? . . . Why not come
> out? Scared? Going to die in the jungle? If you're alive,
> and you think you're a man, take a chance. . . . Onoda's
> brother and a few other Japanese, including me, are
> going to stay in the jungle on Hill 600, without any
> other men. Don't worry about a thing; just come see
> us. . . . We're going to stay in the jungle about a month.
> If we don't get any sign from you during that time, we'll
> be finished. We can't keep on calling for missing men all

our lives. . . . You may be staying out there and feeling
fine, but think how your family feels. Family? That isn't
the whole of it. The Japanese government and everybody in Japan have been worrying about you. More than
that, we are bothering the Philippine government and
the people on this island. You just come out, and everything will be fine. Everybody will be happy, and you
can start a new life. If you're a man, you know what to
do. If you're alive, just answer everybody's expectations.
I beg you. Think, and come out.

Dr. Onoda had written:

Kan, your brother's coming to Lubang again. A few
days after these leaflets are dropped from an airplane,
I'll be right there. I just can't wait. Five months ago,
Mr. Miura, along with your wartime mate Fujita, made
a valiant effort to get in touch with you, carrying heavy
equipment to broadcast to you. They marched through
the jungle for nearly two months, being stung by bees
and oppressed by the heat. . . . At last, the rainy season
is over and it's our turn. . . . Five years ago . . . the Philippine government tried to make you surrender, but that
ended in the unfortunate accident of Shimada's death
on May 7th . . . the very day your uncle Seisaburo was
killed in a traffic accident. . . . If you didn't shoot yourself after that . . . you must be on the island. I'll keep
on crying out with all my voice. . . . We are, in a sense,
messengers to you, chosen from the entire Japanese
people. Kan—and Mr. Kosuka—let's meet, and make all
Japanese, and your parents, of course, feel at ease.

Itagaki figured that Onoda and Kosuka, if they were
anywhere, were probably in the most dense and inac-

cessible part of Lubang—that is, in the vicinity of Hill
600, so named because it is six hundred metres high.
Itagaki deployed most of his men around the edge of the
jungle that shrouds this hill. Then, with the two men's
brothers, Akatsu, and a few bearers, he headed into the
steep thicket, laden with flags, letters, pictures, and bee-
proof face nets. The group stayed there, as Kosuka's
brother had pledged, for twenty-five days. They en-
countered pigs, armadillos, centipedes, and red ants but
not the tiniest shred of evidence of the presence of other
human beings. On November 26th, they gave up. In
Manila, a few days later, Itagaki declared sorrowfully that
he was positive the two men were dead, and he added
that "we are going to take back to Japan their souls and
the memory of the friendship and full cooperation ex-
tended to us by the Philippine Constabulary and the
kindness of the people of Lubang Island. We have done
the best we could." He and his companions also took
back a handful of Lubang pebbles. In Japan, pebbles are
often deemed sacred, and some shrines sell them to
sightseers, as souvenirs, at fifty yen, or about fifteen cents,
a stone. The Lubang pebbles were to be buried in
Onoda's and Kosuka's graves.

On December 11, 1959, the Welfare Ministry decreed that Onoda and Kosuka had died on May 8, 1954,
the day after Shimada was shot. A few days later, funeral
services were held for both men. Concurrently, a popular
Japanese weekly magazine published an article asserting
that those involved in the search had been the victims
of a cruel hoax. The story said that it was well known on
Lubang that Onoda and Kosuka had died in 1954, but

that the inhabitants of the island had nurtured the myth of their survival because they were poor and hoped to profit from the openhandedness of Japanese and Filipino search expeditions. The chief conspirator, the article asserted, was a Philippine Constabulary captain who had commanded the Lubang detachment. He was a convenient fall guy; he had been shot to death himself, by a crazed Filipino soldier, some months earlier, and couldn't issue a rebuttal. General Campo denounced the story as preposterous and libellous, and, as if in defiance of it, promptly sent still another search party to Lubang, with explicit orders "to seek, kill, and/or capture the reported two (2) Jap stragglers." The Constabulary unit spent two months at its task, and on February 15, 1960, its commander concluded, hedgingly:

> No positive indication confirming either the presence or death of the Jap stragglers was found by the units in the entire duration of operation, hence a positive determination as to whether the Jap stragglers are still alive or are already dead cannot be made. The mere fact that the operation did not encounter or find the Japanese or any indication thereof, is not conclusive findings that they are dead already. This is further reinforced by the fact that neither was there any trace, evidence and/or indications found by the troops to make a positive showing that the stragglers are already dead. Not a single piece of equipment like their utensils, firearms, and clothing which are expected to be abandoned if they are dead already was found by the units in spite of sincere efforts made to locate them. Most significant is the fact that no skeletal remains of the two was found.

Actually, the Constabulary hadn't come back quite empty-handed. For its sincere efforts, it did have to show four Japanese helmets, a pair of rotting shoes, a canteen, an indecipherable Japanese dog tag, and a few skeletal remains: human bones identified as those of a male approximately five feet one inch tall—a statistic that was inconclusive, since while both Onoda and Kosuka were of short stature, so were most of the other Japanese who'd gone to Lubang, and so also were most of the island's permanent residents.

Tranquillity had by no means come to Lubang. On January 26, 1961, two Filipinos were shot there, one mortally, and a week later the Manila *Daily Bulletin* chanted the old editorial refrain about the need to have such depredations firmly attributed either to stragglers or to less glamorous outlaws. "There are strong reasons, among them the right of people on Lubang to expect protection from the government, for the authorities to end once and for all the mystery of the Japanese stragglers on the island," said the *Bulletin*. "Lubang is not such a vast expanse as to require our entire armed forces to comb it thoroughly for any remnants of the Japanese Army and restore peace and order. . . . Most people are beginning to feel that it is about time to put a stop to reports on Japanese stragglers and their forays into peaceful settlements."

On February 15, 1961, eleven days after the editorial appeared, two highway laborers on Lubang were shot and killed. One, as he was dying, said he'd had a glimpse of a Japanese uniform. Less than a month after *that*, on March 8th, a Lubang farmer and his two sons were attacked while they were resting in their hut. The father was fatally wounded. The sons reported that the assailants were Japanese stragglers—"tall, healthy, with long hair and white complexions." (Onoda and Kosuka were not only short but also comparatively dark-skinned.) Once again the Constabulary beat the bushes of Lubang. Once again it found nothing. When Itagaki and his associates at the Repatriation Section were apprised of these shootings, they merely shrugged. Dr. Onoda, after hearing the news at his hospital in Tokyo, said, "I no longer care about straggler stories. Whatever may have happened, it can't have been my brother's doing. He's already dead." But, the doctor added, if any really *reliable* information about stragglers should emanate from Lubang, he would be willing to go back there a third time to look for Hiro-chan. On February 11, 1962, a Lubang farmer—whose reliability is hard to evaluate—reported that he saw two armed men in old Japanese Army uniforms enter the village of Tiling, where two natives were subsequently killed, and a house was burned down. The legend lived on. Meanwhile, Lieutenant Onoda's mother continued to serve her absent son his daily meals.

ABOUT THE AUTHOR

A staff writer for *The New Yorker* since his graduation from Harvard in 1937, E. J. KAHN, JR., has contributed reports to that magazine from such far-off spots as Australia, New Guinea, Panama, Germany, Russia, Japan, Korea and Alaska. He is the author of nine books and the father of three sons.